# St. Paul
# Family
# Catechism

## Truths—Sacraments
## Moral Teachings
## Prayer

By a Team of the Daughters of St. Paul

Introduction by
HIS EXCELLENCY,
MOST REVEREND PIO LAGHI
*Apostolic Delegate to the United States*

ST. PAUL EDITIONS

NIHIL OBSTAT:

Rev. Richard V. Lawlor, S.J.
*Censor*

IMPRIMATUR:

✠ Humberto Cardinal Medeiros
*Archbishop of Boston*

**Library of Congress Cataloging in Publication Data**

Main entry under title:

St. Paul family catechism.

Bibliography: p.
Includes index.
1. Catholic Church—Catechisms—English.
I. Daughters of St. Paul. II. Title: Saint Paul family catechism.
BX1961.S7        1983        238'.2        83-18828

ISBN 0-8198-7329-2 cloth
     0-8198-7330-6 paper

Unless otherwise indicated, the Scripture quotations in this publication are from the Revised Standard Version Bible (modified form), Catholic Edition, copyrighted © 1965 and 1966 by the Division of Christian Education of the National Council of the Churches of Christ in the U.S.A., and used by permission.

Scripture verses designated New American Bible (NAB) were taken from: *The New American Bible,* © 1970, used herein by permission of the Confraternity of Christian Doctrine, copyright owner.

Excerpts designated Jerusalem Bible (JB) were taken from: *The Jerusalem Bible,* copyright © 1966 by Darton, Longman & Todd, Ltd. and Doubleday and Company, Inc. Used by permission of the publisher.

Excerpts from the English translation of the *Rite of Penance* © 1974, International Committee on English in the Liturgy, Inc. (ICEL); excerpts from the English translation of *Pastoral Care of the Sick: Rites of the Anointing and Viaticum* © 1982, ICEL. All rights reserved.

Cover credit: DSP

Printed in the U.S.A. by the Daughters of St. Paul
50 St. Paul's Ave., Boston, MA 02130

The Daughters of St. Paul are an international congregation of religious women serving the Church with the communications media.

# CONTENTS

TO THE HOLY FAMILY OF NAZARETH
JESUS, MARY AND JOSEPH:
That they may teach all families
the sanctity of human love
and the value of family life
lived in joy and peace;
that they may strengthen them
to face the troubles of life
bring their hopes to fulfillment
and finally grant them
the eternal happiness of heaven.

# INTRODUCTION

At a symposium held both at Paris and Lyons in January of 1983, Cardinal Joseph Ratzinger, the Prefect of the Sacred Congregation for the Doctrine of the Faith, made the following opening statement in his address entitled, "Transmission of the Faith and the Sources of the Faith":

The final word addressed by the Lord to His disciples charged them to go into the whole world and make disciples of all men (Mt. 28:19ff.; Lk. 16:15; Acts 1:7). What pertains to the very essence of the Faith is this injunction that it is to be handed on—this means the interiorization of a message which is addressed to all because it is the truth and because man cannot be saved apart from the truth (1 Tm. 2:4). This is why catechesis and the handing on of the Faith have been from the beginning a basic responsibility for the Church, and they must continue to be so for as long as the Church continues to exist.

11

It has been the constant teaching of the Church that this responsibility to catechize extends to those whom the Church regards as the first educators of children, namely: their parents. Pope John Paul II has recently stated:

Education in the Faith by parents, which should begin from the children's tenderest age, is already being given when members of a family help each other to grow in faith through the witness of their Christian lives, a witness that is often without words but which perseveres throughout a day-to-day life lived in accordance with the Gospel.... Christian parents must strive to follow and repeat, within the setting of family life, the more methodical teaching received elsewhere. The fact that these truths about the main questions of faith and Christian living are thus repeated within a family setting impregnated with love and respect will often make it possible to influence the children in a decisive way for life (*Catechesi tradendae*, no. 68).

The Daughters of St. Paul are to be commended for the publication of their *Saint Paul Family Catechism*. This invaluable catechetical tool, modeled after the great catechisms that have been a part of the Catholic Church's tradition, will enable parents to meet their educational responsibilities more effectively. The concise and precise question-and-answer format will facilitate the student's ability to learn the Church's fundamental teachings.

It is my fond hope that this volume will be greeted warmly by every parent who takes seriously the God-given right to educate his or her children in the Faith.

*Pio Laghi*

ARCHBISHOP PIO LAGHI
Titular Archbishop of Mauriana
Apostolic Delegate in the United States

Washington, D.C.
September 28, 1983

*Part One*

# Principles of
# Family Catechetics

"Jesus saw a vast crowd. He pitied them; for they were like sheep without a shepherd; and he began to teach them at great length" (Mk. 6:34).

**"On another occasion he [Jesus] began to teach beside the lake. Such a huge crowd gathered around him that he went and sat in a boat on the water, while the crowd remained on the shore nearby. He began to instruct them at great length..." (Mk. 4:1-2).**

There is nothing new about family catechetics. Jesus, the Divine Master, often put Himself in the midst of families to instruct them in the Good News of salvation. When He taught in the synagogues, as the Gospels tell us He did, we can assume the audience to have been mainly adult, and probably men. But when He taught the crowds in the Temple precincts, on the hillsides or along the lakeshore, we can envisage entire families seated together listening to the Word of Truth. How easy to imagine a mother explaining still further to her little ones so that not one word would go lost from their open, eager minds. This was the crowd that Jesus loved; the crowd that constantly sought Him out to listen to His teaching; the crowd that He fed miraculously with the loaves and fishes—a crowd made of countless ordinary families.

The divine method does not change. The parables and the teachings that came from the mouth of the Incarnate Word are meant just as much for today's families as for those of long ago. The simplicity of the language used by the Son of God shows a master Teacher who could hold spellbound fishermen, traders and tax collectors, as well as women and children. He filled hungry minds with truth; He caused people to change their way of life as they tried to practice what He taught; He caused hearts to seek union with the living God, their Father and Creator. Jesus Master is the model Catechist, the first Catechist to the family.

> Jesus did not come to teach us astronomy or geography, but He came to teach us the way to heaven. Jesus left geography, arithmetic and all the other natural sciences to men, to regular school teachers. However, He reserved for Himself the greatest science, the most necessary, the most certain, the one which helps, not for living here, but for living eternally happy up above; if in the schools engineers and teachers, etc., are made, in the school of the Gospel the blessed of heaven are made—the saints, the souls who must not only think of spending a happy life down here, but a happy life eternally up above.[1]

From the beginning of His ministry, Jesus handpicked twelve men to be closely associated with Him. They gathered around Him as students around a teacher and accompanied Him in His travels. These disciples He instructed with painstaking care, constantly explaining and correcting. They were students of the school of the Divine Master and He trained them to carry on His saving work. Each of them was meant to become an apostle, a teacher sent out to instruct men in life-giving truths, who by word and example would show others the way of salvation.

At Jesus' Ascension, the Apostles were still fearful, hesitant men. They did not yet fully resemble their divine Teacher. They gathered around Mary, the Queen of Apostles, drew from her faith and listened to her as she led them to a greater understanding of the teachings of her Son. The Divine Master had promised to send the Holy Spirit, who "will instruct you in everything, and remind you of all that I told you" (Jn. 14:26). And again, "he will guide you to all truth..." (Jn. 16:12). So with Mary they prayed and waited for the fulfillment of the promise.

At Pentecost, with the descent of the Holy Spirit, the Apostles emerged as competent teachers, filled with a burning zeal to share what they had received. After the spectacular events of Pentecost, the Apostles began a systematic missionary endeavor to instruct in the new way all who would listen.

They taught anywhere and everywhere to anyone who would listen. We see them instructing families as their Master had done before them. Peter taught Cornelius, who had "called in his relatives and close friends" (Acts 10:24). It seems that Cornelius and his entire family were involved in both the instruction and the subsequent conversion. We know children were present at some of Paul's preaching when we recall the story of Eutychus. The Acts tells us that "a young lad named Eutychus" was present at one of St. Paul's lengthy instructions and was "sitting on the window-sill" (Acts 20:9).

Religion was a family affair. Parents were expected to train their children in godliness and children were expected to obey. No special classes were held for the children, yet we know they, too, were instructed, for entire families were baptized together. In the Acts of the Apostles we read that when Paul and Silas were in prison in Philippi a miraculous earthquake released them and all the prisoners. The jailor, thinking all had escaped, would have committed suicide. Paul stopped him from harming himself and then "proceeded to announce the word of God to him and to everyone in his house.... Then he and his whole household were baptized" (Acts 16:32-33). It was apparently assumed that the adults would see to the further instruction of the children. As they themselves grew in the Faith their children would also grow in knowledge and understanding. In fact, in Paul's letter to Titus, he lays down as one of the qualities of a presbyter, or priest, that he be "the father of children who are believers" (Ti. 1:6). The parents themselves were appointed as teachers of their children, guardians of their faith and their moral conduct.

As the Church grew in numbers and spread to every part of the then-known world, an organized program developed to impart to new converts the entire Deposit of Faith as it had been received from the first teachers, the Apostles, who, in turn, had received it from the divine Teacher Himself. This organized program was commonly called the catechumenate. It was a systematic catechesis which carefully taught the same truths wherever it was established. Whether it was in Rome or in Alexandria, an identical program was followed.

> [It] was everywhere the same, the same as it had been back to its origin in the teaching of Jesus. Wherever the Catholic Church reached and branched out from these original apostolic centers, it took root and grew by means of this same catechetical program for handing on the faith by teaching.[2]

In the catechumenate, no special provision was made for children. It was a program for adults and geared to adults of various backgrounds. St. Augustine, in *The First Catechetical Instruction*, makes it clear that farmers and intellectual students should receive different treatment but, of course, the same Faith.[3] Children were not counted unimportant. The catechumenate was merely following the tradition of the Church in obliging parents to see to the instruction of their children. Infant Baptism was the normal course and introduced the child into the family of God. Parents originally stood as sponsors and answered for their child, reciting the Apostles' Creed. It was taken for granted that the child would be raised in such a way as to grow in wisdom, age and grace.

Father Jungmann states that in the catechumenate,

> there can be found no trace of an ecclesiastical catechesis for baptized children. It was considered normal for parents to undertake the further religious training of their children. The children grew into the religious life of the Church through assistance at Mass.[4]

That the parents were the primary educators of their children was taken for granted by the Church. Father Johannes Quasten tells us that St. John Chrysostom

>...urges parents to regard the education of their children as the highest and holiest of tasks and to provide them with the true riches of the soul rather than with worldly wealth. They must train their boys and girls not for time, but for eternity.[5]

And, in another place, St. John Chrysostom tells parents:

>In children we have a great charge committed to us. Let us bestow great care upon them, and do everything that the Evil One may not rob us of them.[6]

Around the 6th century, the great majority of Catholics entered the Church as infants at the baptismal font, and the catechumenate had practically ceased to function. Catechetical instruction was imparted by means of sermons at the Sunday liturgy and at other liturgical devotions. Religion was still a family affair and entire families attended Mass. In later centuries, families would also listen to the itinerant preaching of Franciscans and Dominicans. Children depended almost exclusively on their parents' explanations. Many parishes began to develop some special instructions for sacramental preparation, but even here, parents held a primary role. Advent and Lent were often the times chosen for this special preparation which culminated in the reception of the Sacraments of Penance and Holy Communion.

At no time in the history of the Church was the religious education of children in general neglect. Various local councils obliged parish priests to instruct the children of their parish. Fathers McHugh and Callan in their Introduction to *The Catechism of the Council of Trent* list a number of these councils. They mention, besides these "parish schools," episcopal schools and monastic centers for the education of the children in the locality, convent schools for girls and even other schools operated by nuns for all the children of a village.[7] In these various schools children were taught to read and write and the religious instruction they were receiving at home was reinforced. These schools never sought to replace the essential role of the parents as far as the religious education of the children was concerned.

The Popes of the 19th and 20th centuries have found special cause continually to restate the Church's teaching on the right and obligation of parents in the education of their children. As education was more and more wrenched from the Church and entrusted to the state, it became more and more common for parents' rights to be overlooked at the least, and actually suppressed at the worst. Some parents themselves tended to forget their role as educators as they saw schools become more sophisticated in imparting secular learning. Pope Pius IX, in 1864, found it necessary to warn against the separation of religion from public education and from family life.[8]

Pope Pius XII spoke and wrote extensively on family catechesis. In his numerous addresses to newlyweds and married couples, he frequently recalled their sublime role as educators of their children. He never tired of condemning the dangers of atheistic communism to family life. He continually reminded parents of their sacred duties and reminded the State that it could in no way rob parents of their God-given obligations. His primary concern was Christian education properly so-called, not just social and civil education. He clearly stated in an address to the men of Catholic Action:

> Greatly deserving of praise from the Church and society are they who, permeated by their great responsibility, undertake to be the first educators of their own children by word and example, educating them in the Christian doctrine and its daily practice.[9]

In our own times we have received from the heart and the pen of Pope John Paul II probably the most lengthy Apostolic Exhortation ever released by a Pope: *Familiaris consortio*. The English title clearly delineates the contents—"The Role of the Christian Family in the Modern World." As one would expect, the principle of parents as the primary religious educators of their children is covered in great detail. Number 38 states:

> For Christian parents the mission to educate, a mission rooted, as we have said, in their participation in God's creating activity, has a new specific source in the sacrament of marriage, which consecrates them for the strictly Christian education of their children: that is to say, it calls upon them to share in the very authority and love of God the Father and Christ the Shepherd, and in the motherly love of the Church, and it enriches them with wisdom, counsel, fortitude and all the other gifts of the Holy Spirit in order to help the children in their growth as human beings and as Christians.[10]

By word and example children should see in their parents an example of what to believe, how to live and how to pray. Evangelization cannot be reserved for those outside the Catholic Faith, or left up to those who have chosen the priestly or religious life. Evangelization, like charity, begins at home and proceeds from there or does not proceed at all.

In *Evangelii nuntiandi*, it is said:

> The family, like the Church, ought to be a place where the Gospel is transmitted and from which the Gospel radiates. In a family which is conscious of this mission, all the members evangelize and are evangelized. The parents not only communicate the Gospel to their children, but from their children they can themselves

receive the same Gospel as deeply lived by them. And such a family becomes the evangelizer of many other families, and of the neighborhood of which it forms a part.[11]

Pope John Paul II has made it clear that in today's consumer society, the family can become the most "suitable place to revive the faith." In modern man's psychology, the most "sacred place" seems to be the home, even as it was in apostolic times.[12] The home still remains the ideal place for safeguarding faith and morals and for the formation of a Christian character. The Jesuit catechist, Johannes Hofinger, considers the parents' role irreplaceable:

> They are the first and foremost educators of their children. Their role is so decisive that scarcely anything can compensate for their failure in it. It is within the family that children first learn to know God, to worship Him, and to love their neighbor.[13]

If parents carefully guard the material and cultural heritage of their children, how much more should they guard their spiritual heritage as found in our holy Catholic Faith! The Church has been entrusted by her Founder with a divine Deposit of Faith. Parents in turn are the trustees of this Deposit of Faith for their children. In what does the Deposit of Faith consist? In all that Christ taught and that the Church continues to teach through her ordinary and extraordinary Magisterium. The Deposit of Faith is divine revelation in all its fullness. It is this Deposit of Faith that constitutes the content of family catechetics.

> The mission to educate demands that Christian parents should present to their children all the topics that are necessary for the gradual maturing of their personality from a Christian and ecclesial point of view.[14]

*The Declaration on Christian Education* from Vatican Council II describes the content of Christian formation as follows:

> A Christian education does not merely strive for the maturing of a human person...but has as its principal purpose this goal: that the baptized, while they are gradually introduced to the knowledge of the mystery of salvation, become ever more aware of the gift of Faith they have received, and that they learn in addition how to worship God the Father in spirit and truth (cf. Jn. 4:23) especially in liturgical action, and be conformed in their personal lives according to the new man created in justice and holiness of truth (Eph. 4:22-24); also that they develop into perfect manhood, to the mature measure of the fullness of Christ (cf. Eph. 4:13) and strive for the growth of the Mystical Body....[15]

The Church has not left parents on their own to discover for themselves the content of the Deposit of Faith. There have been, in the history of the Church, a number of official catechetical texts which are summaries of the basic elements of Christian doctrine. These official catechetical texts were made and enacted by the bishops in their function as chief catechists of their people. For English-speaking Catholics, perhaps the most influential of these are the *Baltimore Catechism, The Catechism of Christian Doctrine* of Pope Saint Pius X, and *The Roman Catechism* of the Council of Trent. *The General Catechetical Directory* states that "greatest importance must be attached to catechisms published by ecclesiastical authority."[16]

*The Baltimore Catechism* was a result of the Third Plenary Council of Baltimore in 1885. Its four hundred and twenty-one questions and answers were arranged in thirty-seven chapters. Most people are more familiar with the 1941 revision made by the bishops' committee of the Confraternity of Christian Doctrine. Father F. J. Connell, C.SS.R., was mainly responsible for this revised edition. Generations of faithful Catholics were "raised on *The Baltimore Catechism*" and found in its formulations a trustworthy expression of the Deposit of Faith. Parents had at hand an official aid in their efforts as the first catechists of their children.

Pope St. Pius X first wrote his *Catechism of Christian Doctrine* in 1905. This official cate-

chism was obligatory for all the dioceses of
Italy and the Pope personally used it to teach
catechism.

> On the basis of this experience, he caused a
> new and final edition of his *Catechism of Christian
> Doctrine* to be published in 1912, with fewer
> points of doctrine, and with the answers ex-
> pressed still more briefly and simply.[17]

This catechism had relatively little influence in
America until more recently. In 1975 a new
translation from the Italian original was made
by Rev. Msgr. Eugene Kevane and was published by Notre Dame Institute Press. Thus
this little work is once again available to the
English-speaking world.

By far the most universally influential
official catechism is *The Roman Catechism*.
Popes and Councils have continually recommended it and quoted from it. Leo XIII recommended that all priests have it close at hand,
and most recently Pope John Paul II wrote in
*Catechesi tradendae* that *The Roman Catechism* "is
a work of the first rank as a summary of
Christian teaching and traditional theology for
use by priests."[18]

*The Roman Catechism* was first published
in 1566 by order of Pope Pius V. It had been
occasioned by the Protestant revolt and the
teachings being spread by a Protestant catechism published by Martin Luther. However,

*The Roman Catechism* was not written in a defensive style. It is a calm, studied and clear presentation of the same content taught by the Apostles and Fathers of the Church. It is and was meant to be an instrument for preserving intact the Deposit of Faith. It deliberately sets forth the ordinary universal Magisterium of the Church. One of the main writers of the catechism was St. Charles Borromeo, a master catechist and giant in the Faith.

*The Roman Catechism* was written primarily as a handbook for priests. It is meant to be a tool for an organic and systematic instruction in the Faith on all levels—the same type of systematic instruction that was given in the early Church. The catechism is divided into four areas, based on the four areas of teaching in the ancient catechumenate: the twelve articles of the Apostles' Creed; the seven sacraments; the ten commandments; and prayer, based on the Our Father. Thus the life of the Catholic is not left up to chance in any area. The revealed truths, the means of grace, the rules of Christian morality and prayer are all given very detailed explanation. The present work follows the same general order as *The Roman Catechism.*

The Synod Fathers themselves "expressed the hope that a suitable *catechism for families* would be prepared, one that would be clear, brief and easily assimilated by all."[19]

Today, when so many parents look for a simple yet complete catechism, this present work will help them to instruct their children. Family catechesis, according to Pope John Paul II, "precedes, accompanies and enriches all other forms of catechesis."[20] No aid and "no text can take the place of a live communication of the Christian message,"[21] but it can certainly make this transmission easier and more systematic.

Guzman Carriquiry, in commenting on *Catechesi tradendae*, notes three levels of catechetical action in the family. The first level is the atmosphere itself of a Christian home. It is the practice of charity and patience among family members, and the day-to-day witness of a Christian life in which each member helps each other member grow in faith. In such a family; Gospel values permeate the common everyday happenings and color both sad and happy events with a Christian light.

The second level occurs in particular family events that give an opportunity for the parents to explain the religious content of these events: the birth of a new child, a Baptism or marriage, the celebration of First Penance and Holy Communion, the reception of Confirmation, special anniversaries, family feasts, and even sad events such as an illness or death in the family. In such events parents are presented with an ideal situation in which to deepen their children's understanding of God's providential care in our lives. It is at this level that family worship and prayer can take on a catechetical meaning and can become treasured moments of growth in faith and in God's grace.

The third level concerns actual catechesis and therefore could require the use of a family catechism. As has already been pointed out, *Evangelii nuntiandi*, when it refers to catechesis, stresses

> that "the intelligence, especially that of children and young people, needs to learn through systematic religious instruction the fundamental teachings, the living content of the truth which God has wished to convey to us and which the Church has sought to express in an ever richer fashion during the course of her long history" (no. 44).

> Clearly, "the methods must be adapted to the age, culture and aptitude of the persons concerned; they must seek always to fix in the memory, intelligence and heart the essential truths that must impregnate all of life" (no. 44).

As John Paul II insists, parents are called to contribute to this "more systematic and organic" catechetical formation. However important the witness of Christian life in the family, it would be "quite useless to campaign for the abandonment of serious and orderly study of the message of Christ in the name of a method concentrating on life experience" (CT 22). Neither will it do to be satisfied with a family contribution through occasional, improvised and fragmentary catechesis, limited to expecting organic systematization and deepening to be given in other, extra-familial settings.

The three levels referred to above are interconnected in a crescendo of catechetical commitment in the Christian family. In this way it is possible "to influence the children in a decisive way for life" (CT 68).[22]

Especially if a child attends public school does the parents' task become more urgent and absolutely vital to the child's religious and moral training. Once a foundation is laid, only an atmosphere of prayer and good example can assure its permanence. A sacramental life lived by both parents and children is the guarantee of an active, growing faith. Where there is family prayer, there is unity and harmony. Religious and moral education are best given when the Christian life is being lived as a constant witness to the truth of the knowledge imparted. When a child can see faith, hope and charity being practiced, it is easier to grow in those virtues. When the sacraments are received regularly and with fervor, it is easy to grow into living a sacramental life. When the holy Sacrifice of the Mass is loved and joyfully participated in, it more readily takes on meaning and importance for the child.

The present family catechism which comprises Part II of this work is based on the official catechetical texts of the Church. Certain other questions and answers not found in the official catechisms reflect present-day needs of today's Catholics.

Key questions are deliberately written in a simple style to make memorization easier. Educators in the secular realm have come full circle concerning the validity of memorization as an educational method.

The use of the memory in religious education remains a valid educational tool and even a necessity unless we are prepared to settle for a "substandard" faith. The desirability of a certain amount of memorization is made clear in number 55 of *Catechesi tradendae:*

> Catechesis has...known a long tradition of learning the principal truths by memorizing.... At a time when, in non-religious teaching in certain countries, more and more complaints are being made about the unfortunate consequences of disregarding the human faculty of memory, should we not attempt to put this faculty back into use in an intelligent and even an original way in catechesis...? Far from being opposed to the dignity of young Christians, or constituting an obstacle to personal dialogue with the Lord, [memorizing] is a real need, as the Synod Fathers forcefully recalled.

Since number 55 of *Catechesi tradendae* mentions the Synod Fathers, it seems appropriate to include here a written intervention by which the episcopal conferences of Canada and the United States expressed themselves at the Synod of Bishops:

> The modern catechetical renewal demands a clear and complete presentation of the content of the faith to children...; a solid presentation, expressed in comprehensible and familiar terms. This facilitates *memorization, which constitutes an important component of education* and which, if integrated well into a program, gives the child a sense of completeness and of mastery, disposes him to be a part of the community of adults by participating in prayer in the family and in the parish, strengthens his identity as a Catholic, and constitutes a reserve of material upon which to fall back in the future (G. Caprile, *op. cit.*, pp. 175-176; the italics is ours).[23]

This intervention is a good example of the opinions that were commonly expressed by the Synod Fathers regarding the need for a certain amount of memorization in the handing on of the Faith.

Parents are the primary but certainly not the only educators of their children.

> The state and the Church have the obligation to give families all possible aid to enable them to perform their educational role properly.... However, those in society who are in charge of schools must never forget that the parents have been appointed by God Himself as the first and principal educators of their children and that their right is completely inalienable.[24]

The right of parents to educate their children is so sacred that not only can it not be taken away from them by force, it also cannot be relinquished. Parents may delegate their authority to various teachers in religious education programs or Catholic schools, but ultimately it is still they themselves who are responsible for the results. Parents should have no qualms of conscience about checking on the religious education program in which their child is enrolled. They should not hesitate to confront the content of such programs with an official catechetical text, or with the requirements set forth in *The General Catechetical Directory* or *Catechesi tradendae*. When discrepancies are found, parents have the right, and even the obligation, to demand that their child receive the fullness of Faith. It is then that they must also double their efforts at home and make their program of family catechetics even more effective.

The education of their children is a God-given right and duty that parents cannot avoid. Responsibility remains even when necessary help is obtained from schools or religious education programs.

The Angelic Shepherd, Pope Pius XII, saw in children the future of the world and the Church. He knew that the children of today are the priests, the religious, the laity, the saints of tomorrow. In speaking to parents about the training children must receive in the home, he ardently reminded them, "What deep and rich potentialities for love, goodness and devotion lie dormant in the heart of a child! You...[parents] must awaken them, direct them, raise them up to Him who will sanctify them, to Jesus, to Jesus and Mary, their heavenly Mother, who will open the child's heart to piety, will teach it to feel compassion for the poor and unhappy. How joyous is the springtime of childhood!"[25]

And how joyous is the task of parents to make Jesus Christ, the Divine Master, the very center and source of this springtime of life!

## FOOTNOTES

1. James Alberione, S.S.P., S.T.D., *Blessed Are the Imitators of Mary Who Bring Jesus to the World* (Boston: Saint Paul Editions, 1982, private publication), p. 30.

2. Eugene Kevane, Introduction to *Teaching the Catholic Faith Today*, Documents of the Holy See (Boston: St. Paul Editions, 1982), p. xxiii.

3. St. Augustine, *First Catechetical Instruction* (Westminster, Maryland: Newman Press, 1946), p. 30.

4. Joseph Andreas Jungmann, *Handing on the Faith* (New York: Herder and Herder, 1959), p. 9.

5. Johannes Quasten, *Patrology*, Vol. III (Utrecht: Spectrum Publishers, 1966), pp. 465-466.

6. St. John Chrysostom, Homily IX of *Homilies on Timothy*, The Nicene and Post Nicene Fathers Series, Vol. XIII (Grand Rapids, Mich.: William B. Eerdmans Publishing Co., 1976), p. 437.

7. John A. McHugh and Charles J. Callan, Introduction to *The Catechism of the Council of Trent for Parish Priests* (Manila, Philippines: Sinag-tala Publishers, 1974), pp. xiii-xiv.

8. *Ibid.*, p. 49.

9. *Ibid.*, p. 391.

10. Pope John Paul II, *Familiaris consortio* (Boston: Saint Paul Editions, 1981), p. 62.

11. Pope Paul VI, *Evangelii nuntiandi* (Boston: St. Paul Editions, 1975), p. 47.

12. Pope John Paul II, Address "The Mission Is Focused on the Family: Privileged Place for Proclaiming the Gospel" *L'Osservatore Romano*, English Edition, December 20, 1982.

13. Johannes Hofinger, S.J. and Francis J. Buckley, S.J., *The Good News and Its Proclamation* (Notre Dame, Ind.: University of Notre Dame Press, 1968), p. 214.

14. Pope John Paul II, *Familiaris consortio*, p. 63.

15. J. L. Gonzalez, S.S.P., and Daughters of St. Paul, comp., *The Sixteen Documents of Vatican II, Gravissimum educationis* (Boston: St. Paul Editions, 1967), p. 237.

16. Sacred Congregation for the Clergy, *General Catechetical Directory* (Washington, D.C.: United States Catholic Conference, 1971), p. 88.

17. Eugene Kevane, Introduction to *Teaching the Catholic Faith Today*, p. xli.

18. Pope John Paul II, *Catechesi tradendae* (Boston: Saint Paul Editions, 1979), p. 12.

19. Pope John Paul II, *Familiaris consortio*, p. 64.

20. Pope John Paul II, *Catechesi tradendae*, p. 57.

21. Sacred Congregation for the Clergy, *General Catechetical Directory*, p. 89.

22. Guzman Carriquiry, "The Irreplaceable Role of the Family," in *"Going Teach..."*, Coordinator Cesare Bonivento, P.I.M.E. (Boston: St. Paul Editions, 1980), pp. 338-343.

23. Ubaldo Giannetto, S.D.B., "Memorization in Catechetical Teaching," in *"Going Teach..."*, p. 378.

24. Pope John Paul II, *Familiaris consortio*, p. 65.

25. Pope Pius XII, "Training in the Home" in *Education*, ed. by the Benedictine Monks of Solesmes, p. 315.

*Part Two*

# Content
# of Family Catechetics

# The Apostles' Creed

FIRST ARTICLE OF THE CREED

**"I believe in God the Father Almighty, Creator of heaven and earth."**

## The Existence and Nature of God

### 1. Who created us?

God created us.

> God created man in his own image,
> in the image of God he created him;
> male and female he created them (Gn. 1:27).

### 2. Who is God?

God is the all-perfect Supreme Being, the Creator of all things, visible and invisible, and who keeps them in existence.

> In the beginning God created the heavens and the earth... (Gn. 1:1).

### 3. How do we know that God exists?

We know that God exists because our reason tells us that the universe could only have been created by an infinitely wise, all-powerful, self-existing Being.

Yerkes Observatory, Williams Bay, Wisconsin

"In the beginning God created the heavens and the earth" (Gn. 1:1).

> Ever since the creation of the world his invisible nature, namely, his eternal power and deity, has been clearly perceived in the things that have been made (Rom. 1:20).

### 4. How else do we know about God?

We also know about God because He revealed Himself to us.

> In many and various ways God spoke of old to our fathers by the prophets; but in these last days he has spoken to us by a Son... (Heb. 1:1-2).

### 5. What does "Supreme Being" mean?

"Supreme Being" means that God is above all created things, is self-existing, and has all perfections without limit.

### 6. What does "self-existing" mean?

"Self-existing" means that no other being caused God to exist.

### 7. Does God have a body as we do?

No, God does not have a body as we do. He is a pure spirit, with intelligence and free will.

### 8. Is God eternal?

God is eternal, since He had no beginning, will have no end, and will always remain the same.

> Before the mountains were brought forth,
>> or ever you had formed the earth and the world,
>> from everlasting to everlasting you are God (Ps. 90:2).

### 9. Does God ever change?

God is absolutely unchangeable because He is all-perfect and can add nothing to His perfection.

> But you are the same, and your years have no end (Ps. 102:27).

### 10. Is God all-powerful?

God is all-powerful, which means He can do all things.

### 11. Is God everywhere?

God is everywhere, that is, present in every place.

> If I ascend to heaven, you are there!
>   If I make my bed in Sheol, you are there!
> If I take the wings of the morning and dwell
>     in the uttermost parts of the sea,
> even there your hand shall lead me, and
>     your right hand shall hold me
>     (Ps. 139:8-10).

### 12. Is God infinitely wise, holy, merciful and just?

Yes, God is infinitely wise, holy, merciful and just because He possesses all perfection in an infinite degree.

## God, Our Creator

### 13. Why do we call God the Creator of heaven and earth?

We call God the Creator of heaven and earth because absolutely nothing existed until God created everything by His almighty power.

> Of old you laid the foundation of the earth,
> and the heavens are the work of your hands (Ps. 102:25).

**14. Did God have to create the universe?**
Nothing compelled God to create the universe. He is absolutely free in all His actions.

**15. Did God create only material things?**
God did not create only material things, but also the angels, who are pure spirits, and the spiritual soul of every human being.

**16. Does God know everything?**
God does know everything: past, present, and future, our most hidden thoughts, desires, words, actions and omissions.

> Even before a word is on my tongue,
> lo, O Lord, you know it altogether (Ps. 139:4).

**17. Does God care about us?**
Yes, God watches over us with fatherly care.

**18. What do we call God's loving care for us?**
We call God's loving care for us Divine Providence.

**19. Can God ever do evil?**
God can never do evil because He is infinitely good and lovable; God permits evil because He respects our free will and can bring good even from evil.

**20. Is God all-good?**
God is all-good, infinitely lovable, and every good comes to us from His fatherly love.

## The Blessed Trinity

**21. Is there only one God?**
Yes, there is only one God.

> "I am the Lord, and there is no other, besides me there is no God..." (Is. 45:5).

**22. What is meant by the Blessed Trinity?**
By the Blessed Trinity is meant that in God there are three divine Persons: the Father, the Son and the Holy Spirit.

**23. Is the Father God?**
Yes, the Father is God, the first Person of the Blessed Trinity.

**24. Is the Son God?**
Yes, the Son is God, the second Person of the Blessed Trinity.

**25. Is the Holy Spirit God?**
Yes, the Holy Spirit is God, the third Person of the Blessed Trinity.

**26. Are the three divine Persons truly equal?**

The three divine Persons are truly equal, because each totally possesses the one divine nature. Yet They are distinct from one another.

**27. Are we able to understand how the three divine Persons are only one God?**

We cannot understand how the three divine Persons are only one God. This is the greatest mystery of our Faith.

**28. What is a mystery?**

A mystery is a supernatural truth which we cannot completely understand, but which we firmly believe because God has revealed it.

## The Angels

**29. Who are the angels?**

The angels are pure spirits who have no physical body, but have intelligence and free will.

**30. Are the angels superior to us?**

Yes, the angels are more perfect than we are and more like God, because they are pure spirits.

### 31. How do we know angels exist?
We know angels exist through divine revelation, that is, Sacred Scripture and Tradition.

### 32. Are all the angels good?
God made all the angels good; however, when He tested them some remained faithful but others rebelled against Him.

### 33. Did God reward the good angels?
God rewarded the angels who remained faithful by giving them the eternal happiness of heaven, where they see God face to face and adore and love Him.

### 34. Do the good angels care for us?
The good angels pray for us and serve as guardian angels.

> For he will give his angels charge of you to guard you in all your ways (Ps. 91:11).

### 35. What does our guardian angel do?
Our guardian angel protects us from spiritual and material dangers, guides our minds to know what is right, prays for us and presents our prayers to God.

### 36. Who are the devils?
The devils, or evil spirits, are the unfaithful angels who were cast into hell for their disobedience.

...God did not spare the angels when they sinned, but cast them into hell and committed them to pits of nether gloom..." (2 Pt. 2:4).

### 37. Can the devils harm us?

The devils want to harm us by tempting us to offend God, but we can resist them with God's help.

> Be sober, be watchful. Your adversary the devil prowls around like a roaring lion, seeking someone to devour. Resist him, firm in your faith, knowing that the same experience of suffering is required of your brotherhood throughout the world (1 Pt. 5:8-9).

## Man

### 38. What is man?

Man is a creature composed of a material body and a spiritual soul. The soul is made in the image and likeness of God, with intelligence and free will, and it is immortal.

> ...for God created man for
>     incorruption,
> and made him in the image of his own
>     eternity... (Wis. 2:23).

### 39. What do we mean when we say that the soul is immortal?

When we say that the soul is immortal, we mean that it will live forever.

> But the souls of the righteous are in the hand of God,

and no torment will ever touch them.
In the eyes of the foolish they seemed to
    have died,
and their departure was thought to be an
    affliction,
and their going from us to be their destruc-
    tion;
but they are at peace.
For though in the sight of men they were
    punished,
their hope is full of immortality (Wis. 3:1-4).

## 40. How does the soul originate?

Each and every human soul is directly
created by God at the moment of the
conception of the body.

## 41. Why did God create us?

God created us to know, love, and serve
Him, our Creator and Lord, and to love
our neighbor for the sake of God. In this
way we attain to salvation, that is, the
eternal happiness of heaven.

## 42. Why did God make us free?

God made us free so that with His help
we can choose what is good and avoid
what is evil and therefore be rewarded
by Him.

## 43. Which should be given more impor-
tance, our body or our soul?

Both are important. "Saving one's soul"
really means saving one's complete self,
body and soul, for heaven.

## 44. Who were the first human beings God created?

The Bible tells us that the first human beings God created were Adam and Eve, the first parents from whom the entire human race descended.

"You made Adam and gave him Eve his wife as a helper and support. From them the race of mankind has sprung" (Tb. 8:6).

## 45. What was the greatest gift that God gave our first parents?

The greatest gift that God gave our first parents was the gift of sanctifying grace, which means a sharing in the divine life, with the right to heaven.

## 46. What other gifts did God give our first parents?

God gave our first parents superior knowledge, control of the passions by reason, and freedom from suffering and death.

## 47. What are we to believe in regard to human evolution?

We are to believe that human evolution is still a theory and not an established fact. Should it be proven true in the future, then we are to believe that only the body evolved, and with the special help of God.

### 48. What is meant by original sin?

Original sin is the sin transmitted to us from Adam. It is called original because it has been passed down to the whole human race from its origin.

### 49. How do we know that original sin is real?

We know that original sin is real from the Bible and from the teachings of the Church.

### 50. If our first parents were created holy, how could they sin?

Although our first parents were created holy, they still lived by faith, and were not yet in heaven, where a person sees God and can no longer sin. When the devil tempted them, they knowingly and willfully disobeyed God.

### 51. What happened to our first parents as a result of their sin?

Because of their sin our first parents lost sanctifying grace and the right to heaven. They lost their other gifts also, becoming inclined to evil and subject to ignorance, suffering and death.

### 52. In what does original sin consist?

Original sin consists in the absence of sanctifying grace and the right to heaven —gifts which Adam was to have transmitted to his descendants.

### 53. In what other ways does original sin affect us?

Original sin makes us inclined to evil and subject to ignorance, suffering and death.

Through one man sin entered the world and with sin death (Rom. 5:12 NAB).

### 54. Does original sin make our human nature totally corrupt?

Original sin does not make our human nature totally corrupt. Our mind can still know truth and our will is still free. Therefore, we can still do good and avoid evil, but with greater effort and God's help.

### 55. Is God unjust in punishing us for Adam's sin?

God is not unjust in punishing us for Adam's sin because original sin does not deprive us of anything to which we have a right as human beings, but only of the free gifts that God gave our first parents. They lost these gifts for themselves and for us, too.

### 56. Is there any remedy for original sin?

Yes, Jesus Christ, our Savior, died on the cross to redeem us from sin and restore sanctifying grace to us.

**Jesus the Teacher**

Vitale da Bologna

57. **When is original sin removed from our soul?**
Ordinarily original sin is removed by the Sacrament of Baptism.

58. **Is there any remedy for the effects of original sin?**
The effects of original sin may be partially remedied by: Scripture reading, religious instruction, fervent prayer, devout reception of the sacraments, self-denial and obedience to God's law.

59. **Was any human being ever preserved from original sin?**
Only the Blessed Virgin Mary was preserved from original sin from the moment of her conception in view of the merits of Jesus, the Savior of mankind. This privilege is called the "Immaculate Conception."

# SECOND ARTICLE OF THE CREED
## "Jesus Christ His only Son our Lord"

### The Incarnation

60. **What is meant by the "Incarnation"?**
By the "Incarnation" is meant that the Son of God became man to save us.

God so loved the world that he gave his only Son, that whoever believes in him should not perish but have eternal life. For God sent the Son into the world, not to condemn the world, but that the world might be saved through him (Jn. 3:16-17).

**61. What does the name "Jesus" mean?**
The name "Jesus" means "Savior."

**62. What does the name "Christ" mean?**
The name "Christ" means "the anointed" or the chosen one of God.

## True God and True Man

**63. Why is Jesus Christ true God and true man?**
Jesus Christ is true God because He has the same divine nature as God His Father. He is true man because He was born of the Blessed Virgin Mary with a body and soul like ours.

**64. Did Jesus Christ ever sin?**
Jesus Christ was always free from all sin, both original sin and personal sin, because He is God.

"Can any one of you convict me of sin?" (Jn. 8:46 NAB)

**65. How many Persons are there in Jesus Christ?**
There is only one Person in Jesus Christ, the second Person of the Blessed Trinity.

66. **How many natures are there in Jesus Christ?**
There are two natures in Jesus Christ: the divine nature and the human nature.

67. **Was the Son of God always man?**
The Son of God was not always man, but became man at the moment of the Incarnation when He united a human nature to His divine nature.

68. **Do we owe worship to Jesus Christ?**
We owe the same worship to Jesus Christ that we offer to God because Jesus is true God as well as true man.

## THIRD ARTICLE OF THE CREED

### "Conceived by the Holy Spirit, born of the Virgin Mary"

*Son of God and Son of Mary*

69. **When did the Incarnation take place?**
The Incarnation took place on the day of the Annunciation, when the Son of God was conceived in the womb of the Blessed Virgin Mary by the power of the Holy Spirit (cf. Lk. 1:26-38).

70. **Who is the father of Jesus Christ?**
God the Father is the only true Father of Jesus Christ; St. Joseph was His foster

Mary, the Mother of God

father and the spouse of the Blessed
Virgin Mary.

**71. When was Jesus Christ born?**
Jesus Christ was born of the Blessed
Virgin Mary nearly 2,000 years ago in a
poor stable in Bethlehem, and we celebrate His birth on Christmas Day (cf. Lk.
2:1-7).

**72. Why did Jesus Christ choose to be born
poor?**
Jesus chose to be born poor to teach us to
be detached from earthly goods which
do not last and to think more often of the
happiness awaiting us in heaven.

## The Blessed Virgin Mary

**73. Was Mary always a virgin?**
Mary was a virgin before, during and
after the birth of Jesus; this is called her
perpetual virginity.

**74. Why is Mary the Mother of God?**
Mary is the Mother of God because she is
the Mother of Jesus Christ, who is the
second Person of the Blessed Trinity.

**75. Why is Mary the Mother of the Church?**
Mary is the Mother of the Church because
she is the Mother of Jesus Christ, who is
the Head of His Mystical Body which is
the Church.

### 76. What does Mary do for us?

Mary is truly our spiritual Mother, who takes loving care of us as a mother does her child.

### 77. Does devotion to Mary diminish our devotion to Jesus Christ?

No. In honoring Mary we imitate Jesus Christ, who loved her as a Mother. We pray to her so that she will make us know her Son, lead us to Him, and help all mankind to accept Him.

## Jesus' Knowledge

### 78. Did Jesus always know that He was God?

Yes. Even though Jesus has two natures, He is only one Person—the Son of God. Thus, He always knew that He was God.

### 79. Did Jesus know all things—past, present and future?

Yes. As God, Jesus Christ from the moment of His Incarnation and throughout His life knew all things—past, present and future.

## Jesus' Proofs of Divinity

### 80. Did Jesus say that He was God?

Yes. During His public life Jesus said that He was God.

So the Jews gathered round him and said to him, "How long will you keep us in suspense? If you are the Christ, tell us plainly." Jesus answered them, "...I and the Father are one." The Jews took up stones again to stone him (Jn. 10:24-25, 30-31).

### 81. Did Jesus prove that He was God?

Yes. Jesus proved that He was God by the miracles that He worked through His own power, by His prophecies, by His holiness of life, by His sublime teachings and especially by rising from the dead.

## Jesus' Private and Public Life

### 82. What did Jesus do during His private and public life?

During His private or hidden life, Jesus gave us an example of hard work and prayer; during His public ministry, He showed us the way to heaven by teaching us how to know, love and serve God.

### 83. How can we follow Jesus?

We can follow Jesus by trying to think as He did, imitating His virtues, and seeking always to grow in His grace.

## FOURTH ARTICLE OF THE CREED

### "Suffered under Pontius Pilate, was crucified, died and was buried"

**The Pietà**

Michelangelo

## The Sufferings and Death of Our Redeemer

84. **What do we mean when we call Jesus Christ our Redeemer?**

When we call Jesus Christ our Redeemer, we mean that He offered Himself to the Father in sacrifice, shedding all His blood for the forgiveness of our sins.

> ...he [Christ] has appeared once for all at the end of the age to put away sin by the sacrifice of himself (Heb. 9:26).

85. **What did Jesus suffer for us?**

For love of us, Jesus suffered an agony of spirit, sweat blood, was scourged and crowned with thorns, and finally underwent crucifixion and death.

86. **When and where did Jesus Christ die?**

Jesus Christ died on Good Friday, outside the city of Jerusalem on a small hill called Golgotha, or Calvary.

87. **Did Jesus really suffer and die?**

Yes, Jesus really suffered and died. We know this from the historical books of the New Testament and other historical sources of the first century.

88. **Did Jesus suffer and die as God or as man?**

Jesus suffered and died as man—that is, in His human nature—because as God He could neither suffer nor die.

### 89. Was Jesus' death like our own?

The death of Jesus was like that of every human being, because His human soul was really separated from His body. But His divine nature remained united to both His body and His soul.

## Jesus' Love for All

### 90. Did Jesus Christ die for everyone or only for the predestined?

Jesus Christ died for the salvation of all human beings who have ever lived or ever will live.

> This is good, and it is acceptable in the sight of God our Savior, who desires all men to be saved and to come to the knowledge of the truth. For there is one God and there is one mediator between God and men, the man Christ Jesus, who gave himself as a ransom for all (1 Tm. 2:3-6).

### 91. Did Jesus Christ *have to* suffer and die for our sins?

No, Jesus Christ did not have to suffer and die for our sins. He did so of His own free will.

> "For this reason the Father loves me, because I lay down my life, that I may take it again. No one takes it from me, but I lay it down of my own accord" (Jn. 10:17-18).

> ...with his stripes we are healed (Is. 53:5).

92. **Could God have chosen another way to redeem us?**
God could have accepted even the smallest suffering of Jesus as adequate for the redemption of all mankind; every suffering of Jesus had an infinite value, since He is God.

93. **Why, then, did Jesus suffer all the pains of His passion and death?**
Jesus suffered all the pains of His passion and death because He wanted to make full reparation to the Father, teach us how evil sin is and show us how much He loves us.

94. **How can we respond to Jesus' love?**
To respond to Jesus' love, we are to trust in His infinite mercy and forgiveness, receive the Sacrament of Reconciliation with sorrow, and above all participate well in the Sacrifice of the Mass, in which Jesus continually offers Himself to the Father for us and for the whole world.

## FIFTH ARTICLE OF THE CREED

**"He descended into hell, the third day he rose again from the dead."**

William Hole

"My Lord and my God!" (Jn. 20:28)

## Christ's Descent into Limbo

**95. What does "He descended into hell" mean?**

When we say that Jesus descended into hell we mean that after His death on the cross, His body remained in the tomb, while His soul went to a place we call the limbo of the Fathers—that is, of the patriarchs and the other just of the Old Testament.

**96. Why did Christ descend into limbo?**

Christ descended into limbo to show Himself to the souls of the just who were waiting there for redemption.

**97. What did Christ do in limbo?**

In limbo Christ announced to the souls of the just that their time of waiting was over and that He had reopened heaven for mankind.

> ...he went and preached to the spirits in prison (1 Pt. 3:19).

## The Resurrection

**98. What do we mean when we say that on the third day Jesus rose from the dead?**

By this we mean that on the third day Christ united His human body and soul and rose from the dead, as He had foretold.

...for he was teaching his disciples, saying to them, "The Son of man will be delivered into the hands of men, and they will kill him; and when he is killed, after three days he will rise" (Mk. 9:31).

## 99. How do we know that Jesus Christ truly rose from the dead?

We know that Jesus Christ truly rose from the dead because this is a historical fact, witnessed by hundreds of Christ's followers and recorded in Sacred Scripture. The Apostles and millions of early Christian martyrs gave up their lives in defense of this truth.

## 100. Why is Christ's resurrection important?

Christ's resurrection is important because it shows that He is truly God and that therefore we are to believe and do everything He teaches us.

## 101. What did Jesus do after His resurrection?

After His resurrection, Jesus remained on earth for forty days to prove that He had truly risen from the dead and to complete the teaching of His Apostles.

## 102. What importance did the Apostles give to Jesus' resurrection?

The Apostles gave Jesus' resurrection the greatest importance. In fact, the heart of their preaching of the Good News was Jesus' divinity, proven by His resurrection.

### 103. How does the resurrection of Jesus inspire us?

The resurrection of Jesus inspires us in this way: it strengthens our faith and gives us courage to suffer for love of Him, so that one day we may join Him in eternal glory.

> ...if we endure, we shall also reign with him (2 Tm. 2:12).

## SIXTH ARTICLE OF THE CREED

### "He ascended into heaven, and sits at the right hand of God, the Father Almighty."

## *The Ascension*

### 104. What is meant by the words "He ascended into heaven"?

The words "He ascended into heaven" mean that forty days after His resurrection Jesus returned in body and soul to His heavenly Father.

> And when he had said this, as they were looking on, he was lifted up, and a cloud took him out of their sight. And while they were gazing into heaven as he went, be-

hold, two men stood by them in white robes, and said, "Men of Galilee, why do you stand looking into heaven? This Jesus, who was taken up from you into heaven, will come in the same way as you saw him go into heaven" (Acts 1:9-11).

## 105. Why did Jesus ascend into heaven?

Jesus ascended into heaven to prepare a place for us as He had promised, to be our Mediator with His heavenly Father, and to send His Holy Spirit to His Apostles.

"And when I go and prepare a place for you, I will come again and will take you to myself, that where I am you may be also" (Jn. 14:3).

For Christ has entered…into heaven itself, now to appear in the presence of God on our behalf (Heb. 9:24).

"…it is to your advantage that I go away, for if I do not go away, the Counselor will not come to you; but if I go, I will send him to you" (Jn. 16:7).

## 106. Did Jesus ascend into heaven alone?

No, Jesus took with Him to heaven all the souls of the just who were in limbo.

## The Power of Jesus

## 107. What does "sits at the right hand of God the Father Almighty" mean?

When we say Christ sits at the right hand of God the Father Almighty, we mean that as God, He has the same power as the Father, and that as man, He is King over all creation.

> If then you have been raised with Christ, seek the things that are above, where Christ is, seated at the right hand of God (Col. 3:1).

## 108. Is Jesus only in heaven now?

As God, Jesus is everywhere; as God and man, He is in heaven and in the Holy Eucharist.

# SEVENTH ARTICLE OF THE CREED

## "From thence He shall come to judge the living and the dead."

## 109. What does "from thence He shall come to judge the living and the dead" mean?

When we say Christ will come from thence to judge the living and the dead, we mean He will come from heaven at the end of the world to judge everyone who has ever lived.

> "...This Jesus, who was taken up from you into heaven, will come in the same way as you saw him go into heaven" (Acts 1:11).

## 110. How many judgments are there?

There are two judgments: one immediately after our death, called the par-

PDDM

"The Father judges no one, but has given
all judgment to the Son" (Jn. 5:22).

ticular judgment; and the other at Christ's second coming at the end of the world, called the general judgment.

## The Particular Judgment

**111. On what will we be judged?**

We will be judged on the good and evil that we have done (thoughts, desires, words, actions, omissions) from the time that we reached the use of reason.

> The lives of all of us are to be revealed before the tribunal of Christ so that each one may receive his recompense, good or bad, according to his life... (2 Cor. 5:10 NAB).

**112. What will happen to people after their particular judgment?**

After their particular judgment, all people will be rewarded in heaven or punished in purgatory or hell.

**113. Will the reward or punishment be carried into effect immediately after the particular judgment?**

Yes, the reward or punishment deserved by each person will be carried into effect immediately after the particular judgment.

## The General Judgment

**114. Why will there be a general judgment?**

There will be a general judgment so that everyone will see that in His infinite mercy God wanted to save us all and that He was just in punishing the unrepentant and in rewarding those who trusted in His infinite goodness.

**115. Will the same sentence be pronounced at both judgments?**

Yes, the sentence of the last judgment will be the same as that of the particular judgment.

**116. On what will we be judged at the general judgment?**

At the general judgment we will be judged especially on our love for God and neighbor. In fact, in referring to the general judgment Jesus says in the Gospel: "Then the King will say to those at his right hand, 'Come, O blessed of my Father, inherit the kingdom prepared for you from the foundation of the world; for I was hungry and you gave me food, I was thirsty and you gave me drink, I was a stranger and you welcomed me, I was naked and you clothed me, I was sick and you visited me, I was in prison and you came to me.' Then the righteous will answer him, 'Lord, when did we see you hungry and feed you, or thirsty and give you a drink? And when did we see you a stranger and welcome you, or naked and clothe you? And when did we see you sick or in prison and visit you?' And the King will answer them, 'Truly, I say to you, as you did it to one of the least of these my brethren, you did it to me.' Then he will say to those at his left hand, 'Depart from me, you cursed, into the eternal fire prepared for the devil and his angels; for I was hungry and you gave me no food, I was thirsty and you gave me no drink, I was a stranger and you did not welcome me, naked and you did not clothe me, sick and in prison and you did not visit me.' Then they also will answer, 'Lord, when did we see you hungry or thirsty or a stranger or naked or sick or in prison, and did not minister to you?' Then he will answer them, 'Truly, I say to you, as you did it not to one of the least of these, you did it not to me.' And they will go away into eternal punishment, but the righteous into eternal life" (Mt. 25:34-46).

# EIGHTH ARTICLE OF THE CREED
## "I believe in the Holy Spirit"

### *The Divinity of the Holy Spirit*

**117. Who is the Holy Spirit?**

The Holy Spirit is God, the third Person of the Blessed Trinity, proceeding from the Father and the Son from all eternity.

PDDM

"There appeared to them tongues as of fire, distributed and resting on each one of them. And they were all filled with the Holy Spirit" (Acts 2:3-4).

### 118. Is the Holy Spirit equal to the Father and the Son?

The Holy Spirit is God, equal to the Father and the Son. He is almighty, eternal and infinite, as are the Father and the Son.

### 119. How do we know about the Holy Spirit?

Jesus Christ taught us about the existence and nature of the Holy Spirit, placing Him on the same level as the Father and the Son.

> "Go therefore and make disciples of all nations, baptizing them in the name of the Father and of the Son and of the Holy Spirit" (Mt. 28:19).

### 120. Are there other names for the Holy Spirit?

Yes, the Holy Spirit is also called Advocate or Paraclete, Sanctifier, Life-giver, Spirit of Christ, Spirit of Love, Spirit of Truth....

## The Holy Spirit and the Apostles

### 121. When did Jesus promise to send the Holy Spirit?

Jesus promised to send the Holy Spirit on several occasions.

> "And behold, I send the promise of my Father upon you; but stay in the city, until you are clothed with power from on high" (Lk. 24:49).

"But the Counselor, the Holy Spirit, whom the Father will send in my name, he will teach you all things, and bring to your remembrance all that I have said to you" (Jn. 14:26).

"But when the Counselor comes, whom I shall send to you from the Father, even the Spirit of truth, who proceeds from the Father, he will bear witness to me" (Jn. 15:26).

"But you shall receive power when the Holy Spirit has come upon you; and you shall be my witnesses in Jerusalem and in all Judea and Samaria and to the end of the earth" (Acts 1:8).

## 122. When did the Holy Spirit come upon the Apostles in a visible way?

The Holy Spirit came upon the Apostles in a visible way in the form of tongues of fire on the first Pentecost Sunday (cf. Acts 2:1-4).

## 123. What happened to the Apostles when they received the Holy Spirit?

The Apostles received the light to understand everything that Jesus had taught them and the zeal to preach it with love and without fear.

## *The Holy Spirit and the Church*

## 124. What is the role of the Holy Spirit in the Church?

The Holy Spirit lives in the Church as her soul to make her holy by the grace of

Jesus Christ; He enables the Church to teach us without error everything that Jesus taught; He transforms the members of the Church into witnesses for the Lord.

### 125. Will the Holy Spirit always live in the Church?

The Holy Spirit was sent by God the Father and God the Son to live in the Church until the end of the world.

> "And I will pray the Father, and he will give you another Counselor, to be with you for ever" (Jn. 14:16).

### 126. What is the role of the Holy Spirit in our lives?

The Holy Spirit dwells in our souls to make us holy with sanctifying grace. He enlightens our minds to know God; He strengthens our wills to carry out God's will; He sets our hearts on fire to love God and neighbor.

### 127. How should we practice devotion to the Holy Spirit?

We should practice devotion to the Holy Spirit by asking Him to enlighten our minds and strengthen our wills and by responding promptly to His inspirations.

# NINTH ARTICLE OF THE CREED
## "The holy Catholic Church; the communion of saints"

### The Visible Church

**128. What is the Catholic Church?**

The Church is the society of the baptized faithful who believe the same Faith, receive the same sacraments, and obey the Bishop of Rome, the Pope, who is the Successor of St. Peter.

The Church is the communion of life, charity and truth and is used by Christ as an instrument for the redemption of all, sent forth into the whole world as the light of the world and the salt of the earth.

**129. Who founded the Catholic Church?**

Jesus Christ founded the Catholic Church. He brought it into being, structured it, passed on to it His own mission and gave it divine life.

**130. Why did Jesus found the Church?**

Jesus founded the Church to continue His work of redemption for all time.

"Go therefore and make disciples of all nations, baptizing them,...teaching them to observe all that I have commanded you; and lo, I am with you always, to the close of the age" (Mt. 28:18-20).

### 131. How did Jesus Christ found the Catholic Church?

Jesus Christ founded the Catholic Church on St. Peter, whom He set as its rock and foundation and to whom alone in a special way He gave the powers of binding and loosing everything on earth, of strengthening his brethren, and of feeding the whole flock.

> "And I say to thee, thou art Peter, and upon this rock I will build my Church, and the gates of hell shall not prevail against it. And I will give thee the keys of the kingdom of heaven; and whatever thou shalt bind on earth shall be bound in heaven, and whatever thou shalt loose on earth shall be loosed in heaven" (Mt. 16:18-19 CCD).

### 132. Who is the Head of the Church?

Jesus Christ is the invisible Head of the Church.

### 133. Who is the Pope?

The Pope is the Vicar of Christ and the visible head of the Church. He has the supreme power of jurisdiction over the whole Church in matters of faith, morals, discipline and the government of the Church. He is the Successor of St. Peter as Bishop of Rome.

### 134. Why did Jesus Christ give His Church a visible head?

Jesus Christ gave His Church a visible

head to preserve the unity of faith, of worship and of brotherly love among the people of God.

135. **What is meant by the hierarchy of the Church?**
By the hierarchy of the Church is meant the organization of the Church's leaders in different levels of authority: first the Pope, then the bishops....

136. **How can it be proven that Jesus gave a hierarchical organization to His Church?**
That Jesus gave a hierarchical organization to His Church can be proven from Sacred Scripture. He delegated His mission to the Apostles (cf. Jn. 20:21); He gave them the mandate to proclaim His Gospel to the whole world (cf. Mt. 28:19; Mk. 16:15); He passed His authority on to them (cf. Lk. 10:16; Mt. 10:40); He promised them the power of binding and loosing (cf. Mt. 18:18); He transferred to them the priestly powers: to baptize (cf. Mt. 28:19), to celebrate the Eucharist (cf. Lk. 22:19), to forgive sins (cf. Jn. 20:23).

137. **Who are the bishops?**
The bishops are the successors of the Apostles, made by Christ the authentic teachers of the Faith. They take the place of the Apostles in the Church today. Only the power of the Pope is superior to theirs.

...Preach the word, be urgent in season and out of season, convince, rebuke, and exhort, be unfailing in patience and in teaching (2 Tm. 4:2).

### 138. Who are priests?

While all who are baptized participate in the common priesthood of the faithful, nevertheless our Lord instituted a ministerial priesthood in which priests are men ordained by the bishop to share in a special way in the priesthood of Christ, especially by offering the Eucharistic Celebration and by reconciling sinners to God and His Church through the Sacrament of Penance. They collaborate with the bishop and are subject to him. There is an essential difference, and not merely a difference in degree, between the common priesthood of the faithful and the priesthood of Holy Orders.

### 139. Who are deacons?

Deacons are men of truly Christian life, ready for every good work for the salvation of souls. Ordained for a ministry of service, they are the helpers of the bishops and priests, whose authority they obey in fulfilling the duties assigned to them.

### 140. Who are religious?

Religious are men and women chosen through a special call of God for the practice of the evangelical counsels of chastity, poverty, and obedience. They renounce the world and dedicate their whole life to loving God and serving His Church. They imitate the poor, chaste and obedient Christ and live in charity in community life.

### 141. Who founded the religious state?

Jesus Christ Himself founded the religious state with the examples of His life and His teachings.

> The disciples said to him, "If such is the case of a man with his wife, it is not expedient to marry." But he said to them, "Not all men can receive this precept, but only those to whom it is given" (Mt. 19:10-11).

### 142. What did Jesus promise to those who leave all things to follow Him?

To those who leave all things to follow Him, Jesus promised: "And every one who has left houses or brothers or sisters or father or mother or children or lands, for my name's sake, will receive a hundredfold, and inherit eternal life" (Mt. 19:29).

### 143. Who are the laity?

The laity are the sons and daughters of the Church who by the infusion of grace in Baptism become sharers in the Divine Nature and heirs to the kingdom of heaven. They do not belong to the ministerial priesthood or to the religious state. They, too, are called at Baptism to attend to their personal union with Christ and to cooperate for the renewal of the world by penetrating with the spirit of Christ the mentality, customs and laws of society.

## The Church as Mystery

### 144. Are there other names for the Catholic Church?

Yes, the Catholic Church has other names, among them: the Mystical Body of Christ, the People of God, the family of God, the house of God, the bride of Christ, the light of nations, and the universal sacrament of salvation.

### 145. Why is the Church called the Mystical Body of Christ?

The Church is called the Mystical Body of Christ because, as St. Paul tells us, Christ is the Head of the community of believers, and we are all united to Him in the Holy Spirit, as the members of a physical body are united to one another (1 Cor. 12:12, 27).

### 146. Who is the soul of the Church?

The Holy Spirit is the soul of the Church. He remains with the disciples of Jesus for all times in Jesus' place (cf. Jn. 14:16); He binds them in one body (cf. 1 Cor. 12:13); He leads them to all truth (cf. Jn. 16:13); He lives in them as in a temple (cf. 1 Cor. 3:16; 6:19); He helps to preserve the Deposit of Faith entrusted to the Church (cf. 2 Tm. 1:14); He directs Church authorities in their activity (cf. Acts 15:28).

## The Church's Mission

**147. What mission did Jesus Christ give to His Church?**

Jesus Christ gave His Church His very own mission: He willed that the Apostles and their successors, the bishops, with Peter and Peter's Successors at their head, should preach His Gospel faithfully, administer the sacraments, and shepherd His people in love.

**148. From where does the Church draw her teachings?**

The Church draws her teachings from Divine Revelation.

**149. What is Divine Revelation?**

Divine Revelation is what God has spoken to us about Himself, the purpose of our life and His plan of salvation. First, God spoke to us through the prophets in the Old Testament, and then, through His Son Jesus Christ, who brought God's revelation to completion in the New Testament. Jesus Christ, the Son of God made man, told us of the innermost being of God (cf. Jn. 1:1-18); He spoke the words of God (cf. Jn. 3:34); and most of all, He accomplished the work of salvation which His Father gave Him to do (cf. Jn. 5:36; 17:4). The central message of Jesus' revelation was that God is love and is with us to free us from sin and death and to raise us up to life eternal.

Thus, through Divine Revelation, God chose to show forth and communicate Himself and the eternal decisions of His will regarding our salvation. That is to say, He chose to share with us those divine treasures which totally transcend the understanding of the human mind.

Divine Revelation was ended with the last Apostle, St. John. The Church does not accept a new public revelation as pertaining to the divine deposit of faith.

**150. Where do we find Divine Revelation?**
We find God's Revelation in Sacred Scripture and in Sacred (Apostolic) Tradition.

**151. What is Sacred Scripture?**
Sacred Scripture, or the Holy Bible, is

the Word of God written down under the inspiration of the Holy Spirit. (See also questions 866-878.)

## 152. What is Sacred Tradition?

Sacred or Apostolic Tradition is the Word of God entrusted by Christ the Lord and the Holy Spirit to the Apostles, and handed down by them to their successors in its full purity (Jn. 21:25; 2 Tm. 1:13-14; 2:2; 2 Thes. 2:15), so that, led by the light of the Spirit of truth, they may, in proclaiming it, preserve this word of God faithfully, explain it, and make it more widely known.

Therefore, both Sacred Scripture and Sacred Tradition are to be accepted and venerated with the same loyalty and reverence.

## 153. What is the Magisterium?

The Magisterium is the living teaching office of the Church, whose authority is exercised in the name of Jesus Christ. The Roman Pontiff and the Bishops teaching in communion with him, have the task of authentically interpreting the Word of God, whether written or handed down, guarding it scrupulously and explaining it faithfully in accord with a divine commission and with the help of the Holy Spirit.

Thus, Sacred Scripture, Sacred Tradition and the teaching authority of the Church, in accord with God's most wise design, are so joined that all together contribute effectively to the salvation of our souls.

**154. Which are the two forms of the Magisterium?**

The two forms of the Magisterium are:

—the *solemn* or *extraordinary* one, which consists of dogmatic definitions. It adds nothing to Divine Revelation, but only explicates it and creates a new obligation to believe.

—the *ordinary* one, which consists of daily teachings by the Pope, and by the Bishops in communion with him. This ordinary Magisterium is also of divine authority.

## *The Marks of the Church*

**155. How can we know that the Catholic Church is the Church Christ founded?**

We can know that the Catholic Church is the Church Christ founded because it is the only one with the marks or characteristics that Jesus Christ gave to His Church: He made it one, holy, catholic and apostolic.

The Catholic Church is *one* because all its members profess the Faith, participate in the same sacrifice and sacraments, and obey the Vicar of Christ, the Roman Pontiff.

> There is one body and one Spirit, just as you were called to the one hope that belongs to your call, one Lord, one faith, one baptism... (Eph. 4:4-5).

The Catholic Church is *holy* because Jesus Christ, its Founder, and the Spirit who gives it life are holy; because it teaches holy doctrine and gives its members the means of living holy lives, thus giving saints to every age.

> ...Christ loved the church and gave himself up for her, that he might sanctify her, having cleansed her by the washing of water with the word, that he might present the church to himself in splendor, without spot or wrinkle or any such thing, that she might be holy and without blemish (Eph. 5:25-27).

The Catholic Church is *catholic*, or *universal*, because it is sent to all peoples of all ages, for all mankind is called by the grace of God to salvation.

> And he said to them, "Go into all the world and preach the gospel to the whole creation" (Mk. 16:15).

The Catholic Church is *apostolic* because Christ founded her on the Apostles and she has always been ruled by the lawful successors of the Apostles, who faithfully transmit the deposit of Faith taught by the Apostles.

> ...built upon the foundation of the apostles and prophets, Christ Jesus himself being the cornerstone... (Eph. 2:20).

## Indefectibility and Infallibility

**156. What does indefectibility mean?**

Indefectibility means that the Catholic Church will remain until the end of the world as the institution of salvation founded by Christ.

> "And I say to thee, thou art Peter, and upon this rock I will build my Church, and the gates of hell shall not prevail against it" (Mt. 16:18 CCD).

**157. What does infallibility mean?**

Infallibility means the impossibility of falling into error. The perpetual assistance of Christ and of the Holy Spirit guarantees the purity and integrity of the faith and morals taught by the Church.

> "...teaching them to observe all that I have commanded you; and lo, I am with you always, to the close of the age" (Mt. 28:20).

> "And I will pray the Father, and he will give you another Counselor, to be with you for ever..." (Jn. 14:16).

> "When the Spirit of truth comes, he will guide you into all the truth..." (Jn. 16:13).

## 158. Is the Pope infallible?

Yes, the Pope is infallible when he speaks *ex cathedra*, that is, when as shepherd and teacher of all Catholics he defines a doctrine regarding faith or morals to be held by the whole Church. He was promised this assistance in the person of St. Peter: "Simon, Simon, behold, Satan has desired to have you, that he may sift you as wheat. But I have prayed for thee, that thy faith may not fail; and do thou, when once thou hast turned again, strengthen thy brethren" (Lk. 22:31-32 CCD).

## 159. Are the bishops infallible?

Individually the bishops are not infallible. However, they do teach infallibly in an ecumenical council when, with the approval of the Pope, they set forth teachings of faith or morals to be held by the entire Church. The bishops can also teach infallibly when, in union with the Pope, outside an ecumenical council, they all teach the same doctrine of faith or morals.

## 160. Is infallibility the same as impeccability?

No, impeccability means sinlessness. No earthly member of the Church claims this.

**161. Why did Jesus make His Church infallible?**

Jesus made His Church infallible so that she would not compromise with the ideas of changing times nor yield to pressures from within or without, but would teach always and only the Faith entrusted to her by Christ, her Founder (Eph. 4:11-15).

**162. How should Catholics feel toward the Church?**

Catholics are to let themselves be guided by the Church, because she communicates to us the truths and grace which make us holy, according to the teaching of St. Paul, "This is the will of God, your sanctification" (1 Thes. 4:3).

**163. What did Jesus say about those who knowingly refuse to believe the Faith preached by the Church?**

Jesus called for unconditional obedience to the Faith preached by the Church. He made eternal salvation depend on it: "He who believes and is baptized will be saved; but he who does not believe will be condemned" (Mk. 16:16).

**164. What is heresy?**

Heresy is a deliberate denial of one or more truths of the Catholic Faith.

### 165. What is schism?

Schism is a deliberate refusal on the part of a Catholic to submit to the authority of the Pope.

### 166. What is apostasy?

Apostasy is the complete rejection of one's Catholic Faith.

## The Church and Non-Catholics

### 167. Since Jesus Christ founded the Church to continue His mission of salvation, are all people obliged to belong to it?

All are obliged to belong to the Catholic Church in order to be saved. However, those who through no fault of their own do not know that the Catholic Church is the true Church are not guilty in the eyes of God and can be saved if they live a good life and correspond to the graces God gives them.

### 168. What is the difference between the Catholic Church and all the other Christian churches?

Catholics and the members of the other Christian churches are brothers who believe in Jesus Christ, are baptized, and possess in common many means of grace and elements of truth. But our separated brethren are not yet blessed with that unity that Jesus Christ bestowed on His followers. Ecumenism is working and praying for this unity.

"I pray...that all may be one" (Jn. 17:20-21).

### 169. May a Catholic belong to a secret society?

The Church does not encourage Catholics to belong to secret societies, and it forbids Catholics to belong to any secret society that plots against the Church or state or is anti-Catholic in any way.

## Church and State

### 170. What does the Catholic Church claim from the state?

The Catholic Church claims religious freedom—which is necessary in order that she may be faithful to the divine command: "Teach all nations" (cf. Mt. 28:19).

First of all, then, I urge that supplications, prayers, intercessions, and thanksgivings be made for all men, for kings and all who are in high positions, that we may lead a quiet and peaceable life, godly and respectful in every way. This is good, and it is acceptable in the sight of God our Savior, who desires all men to be saved and to come to the knowledge of the truth (1 Tm. 2:1-4).

### 171. Should the state fear the Church?

The state should not fear the Church, but must trust her instead, for by preaching the Gospel the Church forms for the state loyal citizens who are promoters of social peace and progress.

### 172. What can the Church do for the community of nations?

By virtue of her mission of imparting knowledge of the divine and natural law, the Church proclaims the rights of man and contributes to the ensuring of truth, justice, freedom, progress, concord, peace and civilization.

### 173. How does the Church regard the poor and needy?

In imitation of Jesus Christ, her Founder, who was sent by the Father "to bring good news to the poor, to heal the contrite of heart" (Lk. 4:18) and "to seek and to save what was lost" (Lk. 19:10), so too, the Church embraces with love all who are afflicted with human sufferings and does all she can to relieve their needs, striving to serve in them the suffering Christ.

## The Communion of Saints

**174. What do we mean when we say, "I believe in the communion of saints"?**

When we say, "I believe in the communion of saints," we profess our belief that the life of each individual child of God is joined, in Christ and through Christ, to the lives of all other Christians in the unity of the Mystical Body of Christ, which is, as it were, a single mystical person.

**175. Who belong to the communion of saints?**

To the communion of saints belong the faithful on earth who are in the state of grace, the blessed already in heaven, and the suffering souls in purgatory, all united in Jesus Christ and sharing in all the good done in the entire Church.

**176. Can the faithful on earth honor and pray to the blessed in heaven?**

The faithful on earth can and should honor and pray to the blessed in heaven because they are very close to God.

**177. Can the blessed in heaven help the holy souls in purgatory and the faithful still living on earth?**

The blessed in heaven can help the holy souls in purgatory and the faithful still living on earth by their prayers.

### 178. Why do the saints pray for us?

The saints pray for us because they love us in God and want us to be with them one day in heaven.

### 179. Can we help the holy souls in purgatory?

We can help the holy souls in purgatory by our prayers, especially the holy Sacrifice of the Mass, by penance, indulgences, and other good works.

> He also took up a collection, man by man, to the amount of two thousand drachmas of silver, and sent it to Jerusalem to provide for a sin offering. In doing this he acted very well and honorably, taking account of the resurrection. For if he were not expecting that those who had fallen would rise again, it would have been superfluous and foolish to pray for the dead. But if he was looking to the splendid reward that is laid up for those who fall asleep in godliness, it was a holy and pious thought. Therefore he made atonement for the dead, that they might be delivered from their sin (2 Mc. 12:43-46).

### 180. May we ask the souls in purgatory to help us?

Yes, prayer to the souls in purgatory has been a common practice in the Church. It is generally believed that the holy souls can help us and that, in fact, they are eager to do so out of gratitude for the prayers and good works that we offer for their release.

**181. Should we help our fellow pilgrims on earth?**

Yes, we can and must help one another by mutual charity, shown especially by performing the spiritual and corporal works of mercy, because every living person is an actual or potential member of the Mystical Body of Christ.

> Above all hold unfailing your love for one another, since love covers a multitude of sins. Practice hospitality ungrudgingly to one another. As each has received a gift, employ it for one another, as good stewards of God's varied grace (1 Pt. 4:8-10).

## TENTH ARTICLE OF THE CREED

### "The forgiveness of sins"

*Personal Sin*

**182. What does "the forgiveness of sins" mean?**

"The forgiveness of sins" means that Jesus Christ in His infinite mercy has given the Church the power to forgive all sins, no matter how serious they are or how often they have been committed, if the sinner is truly sorry.

> ...he breathed on them, and said to them, "Receive the Holy Spirit. If you forgive the

Moretto da Brescia

"I tell you, her sins, which
are many, are forgiven, for she
has loved much" (Lk. 7:47).

sins of any, they are forgiven; if you retain the sins of any, they are retained" (Jn. 20:22-23).

### 183. What is actual or personal sin?

Actual or personal sin is the sin we ourselves commit by any free and willful thought, desire, word, action or omission which is against the law of God.

> Whoever knows what is right to do and fails to do it, for him it is sin (Jas. 4:17).

### 184. How many kinds of actual or personal sin are there?

There are two kinds of actual or personal sin: mortal and venial.

### 185. What is mortal sin and what are its effects?

Mortal, or deadly, sin is any serious offense against God's law. It deprives the soul of sanctifying grace, destroys the merit of all the person's good acts, and makes the soul deserving of eternal punishment in hell, unless the sinner repents.

> Desire when it has conceived gives birth to sin; and sin when it is full-grown brings forth death (Jas. 1:15).

### 186. When is a sin mortal?

A sin is mortal when the following three conditions are all present: 1) the thought, desire, word, action or omission must be seriously wrong or thought to be seriously wrong; 2) the person knows it is seriously wrong; 3) the person freely gives full consent to doing what he or she knows is seriously wrong.

### 187. What is venial sin?

Venial sin is a less serious offense against God's law, which does not deprive the soul of sanctifying grace, but weakens one's resistance to serious sin and makes the sinner deserving of punishment.

> And do not grieve the Holy Spirit of God, in whom you were sealed for the day of redemption (Eph. 4:30).

### 188. What makes a sin venial?

A sin is venial when it is an offense against God but lacks one or more of the characteristics of a mortal sin.

### 189. What are the effects of venial sin?

Venial sin darkens the mind, weakens the will, lowers one's resistance to temptation and makes the person deserving of punishment in this life and in purgatory.

## Sources and Occasions of Sin

### 190. What are the main sources of sin?

The main sources of sin are the seven capital sins: pride, covetousness or avarice, lust, anger, gluttony, envy, and sloth or laziness as regards spiritual matters.

### 191. What does "capital sins" mean?
"Capital sins" means that these seven vices are the chief sources of actual or personal sins.

### 192. What is the source of all the capital sins?
The source of all the capital sins is original sin.

### 193. What is meant by "occasions of sin"?
By "occasions of sin" is meant persons, places or things which lead one to sin. They are proximate, or near, occasions of sin when they will certainly, or almost certainly, lead a person to sin. They are remote occasions of sin when the danger of sinning is only slight.

### 194. Are we obliged to avoid the occasions of sin?
We are obliged to avoid all the near occasions of sin which we are able to avoid.

### 195. What are temptations?
Temptations are inclinations to sin arising from the world, the flesh, and the devil.

## 196. Can we always resist temptations?

We can always resist temptations, with the grace that God never denies to those who ask Him with confidence.

> No temptation has overtaken you that is not common to man. God is faithful, and he will not let you be tempted beyond your strength, but with the temptation will also provide the way of escape, that you may be able to endure it (1 Cor. 10:13).

## Situation Ethics and Fundamental Option

## 197. What is "situation ethics"?

"Situation ethics" contends that moral decisions should not be based on universal moral laws, but on the specific particular situation in which a person finds himself. Since this situation is unique and unrepeatable, the person's conscience alone is to determine the right moral decision, apart from any universal principle or law. The fundamental error of situation ethics is that it is incompatible with the fact that God gave us an objective norm to judge what is right and wrong: His Ten Commandments. The Church has always taught that there are some acts which are intrinsically good and some which are intrinsically evil, apart from any circumstances.

**198. What is "fundamental option"?**

"Fundamental option" is the theory of those who hold that a person commits a mortal sin only when he has the intention of rejecting God.

**199. What does the Church teach about "fundamental option"?**

The Church teaches that when a person knowingly and willfully does anything which is seriously against God's law, a mortal sin is *always* committed no matter what the sinner's intention is.

## The Sacraments of Forgiveness

**200. How does the Church forgive sin?**

Jesus Christ made the Church the "sacrament of salvation" and gave her two sacraments for the forgiveness of sins after Baptism: Penance, or Reconciliation, and the Anointing of the Sick.

**201. What must we do to keep from sinning?**

To keep from sinning we must pray constantly, receive the sacraments often, remember that God sees us, recall that we are temples of the Holy Spirit, keep busy with work or recreation, promptly resist temptations and avoid the near occasions of sin.

...for once you were darkness, but now you are light in the Lord; walk as children of light... (Eph. 5:8).

Let any one who thinks that he stands take heed lest he fall (1 Cor. 10:12).

# ELEVENTH ARTICLE OF THE CREED
## "The resurrection of the body"
### Bodily Resurrection

**202. What does "the resurrection of the body" mean?**

"The resurrection of the body" means that the bodies of all people will rise from the dead at the end of the world and will be reunited to their souls for all eternity.

> ...we shall all be changed, in a moment, in the twinkling of an eye, at the last trumpet. For the trumpet will sound, and the dead will be raised imperishable, and we shall be changed. For this perishable nature must put on the imperishable, and this mortal nature must put on immortality..." (1 Cor. 15:51-53).

**203. Why will our body rise?**

Our body will rise from the dead so that, together with our soul, it may share in the reward or punishment we have deserved during our life on earth.

**204. How can our body rise to life again?**

God is almighty; He can do all things. Therefore, He can easily resurrect our body. Jesus once said: "I am the resurrection and the life; he who believes in me, though he die, yet shall he live" (Jn. 11:25).

The Church strongly recommends the burial of the bodies of the deceased, but it does not forbid cremation unless it has been chosen for reasons that are contrary to Christian teaching.

### 205. Will each of us have our own body when we rise from the dead?

When we rise from the dead each of us will have the same body we had on earth, but if we have been faithful to God it will be in a glorified state, that is, exceedingly beautiful and forever free from pain and death.

> It is sown in dishonor, it is raised in glory. It is sown in weakness, it is raised in power. It is sown a physical body, it is raised a spiritual body. If there is a physical body, there is also a spiritual body (1 Cor. 15:43-44).

### 206. Has anyone already entered heaven with a glorified human body?

Yes, Jesus Christ is in heaven with His risen glorified body. And His holy Mother Mary was taken up into heaven, body and soul, to share in His happiness, as she had shared in His sufferings.

Sahata

"You made us for Yourself, O Lord,
and our hearts are restless
until they rest in You." —St. Augustine

## Reincarnation

**207. What is meant by "reincarnation"?**

"Reincarnation" is the false teaching that the souls of the dead keep returning to earth in new forms or bodies.

**208. Does the Bible show that reincarnation is a false belief?**

Various Scripture passages show that reincarnation is a false belief. One of these is: "...it is appointed for men to die once, and after that comes judgment" (Heb. 9:27).

# TWELFTH ARTICLE OF THE CREED
## "And life everlasting"

## Eternal Life

**209. What is meant by "life everlasting"?**

"Life everlasting" means the eternal happiness that the blessed will experience in heaven, and the eternal suffering that the wicked will experience in hell.

> "The King will say to those at his right hand, 'Come, O blessed of my Father, inherit the kingdom prepared for you from the foundation of the world....' Then he will say to those at his left hand, 'Depart from me, you cursed, into the eternal fire prepared for the devil and his angels'" (Mt. 25:34, 41).

**210. What is meant by the immortality of the soul?**

The immortality of the soul means that the soul will never die, it will live forever.

## Hell

**211. What is hell?**

Hell is a place where the wicked will be forever deprived of the vision of God and forever punished with every kind of suffering, with no relief.

"...where their worm does not die, and the fire is not quenched" (Mk. 9:48).

**212. Who will be eternally punished in hell?**

They will be eternally punished in hell who have sinned mortally and died without repenting.

"The Son of man will send his angels, and they will gather out of his kingdom all causes of sin and all evildoers, and throw them into the furnace of fire; there men will weep and gnash their teeth" (Mt. 13:41-42).

**213. How can a loving God send anyone to hell?**

God is loving, but is also just, and He respects each person's free will to choose life or death, heaven or hell, by his or her own way of life on earth.

If you will, you can keep the commandments,
and to act faithfully is a matter of your own choice.
He has placed before you fire and water:
stretch out your hand for whichever you wish.
Before a man are life and death,
and whichever he chooses will be given to him (Sir. 15:15-17).

## *Purgatory*

### 214. What is purgatory?

Purgatory is a place where the souls of the just who die with venial sins or with punishment still due for forgiven sin will undergo purification before entering heaven.

### 215. Will purgatory last forever?

No, purgatory will not last forever. After the general judgment there will be only heaven and hell.

## *Heaven*

### 216. What is heaven?

Heaven is a place of everlasting possession and vision of God, in which the souls of the just will be filled with a complete happiness that is totally free from suffering or fear of loss.

...no eye has seen, nor ear heard, nor the heart of man conceived, what God has prepared for those who love him... (1 Cor. 2:9).

I consider that the sufferings of this present time are not worth comparing with the glory that is to be revealed to us (Rom. 8:18).

...it does not yet appear what we shall be, but we know that when he appears we shall be like him, for we shall see him as he is (1 Jn. 3:2).

...and I heard a great voice from the throne saying, "Behold, the dwelling of God is with men. He will dwell with them, and they shall be his people, and God himself will be with them; he will wipe away every tear from their eyes, and death shall be no more, neither shall there be mourning nor crying nor pain any more, for the former things have passed away" (Rv. 21:3-4).

## 217. Who will be eternally rewarded in heaven?

They will be eternally rewarded in heaven who did good works and died in the state of grace, and who are, after their purgatory, free from all venial sin and purified of all punishment due to sin.

"...but lay up for yourselves treasures in heaven, where neither moth nor rust consume and where thieves do not break in and steal" (Mt. 6:20).

"For the Son of man is to come with his angels in the glory of his Father, and then he will repay every man for what he has done" (Mt. 16:27).

## 218. What must we do to attain heaven?

To attain heaven we must fulfill the purpose for which God made us—that is, know, love and serve Him in this life. Those who strive to know, love and serve God better will be rewarded with greater glory.

"And this is eternal life, that they know you the only true God, and Jesus Christ whom you have sent" (Jn. 17:3).

"He who has my commandments and keeps them, he it is who loves me; and he who loves me will be loved by my Father, and I will love him and manifest myself to him" (Jn. 14:21).

...each shall receive his wages according to his labor (1 Cor. 3:8).

## "Amen"

**219. How do we end the Apostles' Creed?**
We end the Apostles' Creed with the word "Amen," which means: *So be it;* that is, *I firmly believe all the truths contained in this prayer,* as revealed by God and taught by the Church.

DSP

"I came that they may have life, and have it abundantly" (Jn. 10:10).

# Divine Grace
## and the Sacraments

### GRACE

## God's Free Gift

**220. What is grace?**

Grace is a supernatural gift freely given to us by God for our eternal salvation. All grace comes to us through the merits of Christ's passion and death and is offered to us by His Church.

**221. Why is grace called a supernatural gift?**

Grace is called a supernatural gift because we have no right to it and it is given to us for a supernatural purpose: the attainment of heaven.

## Sanctifying Grace

### 222. What is sanctifying grace?

Sanctifying grace is a supernatural quality infused into our soul by God to make us holy (cf. 1 Cor. 6:11). By sanctifying grace we share in the divine nature (cf. 2 Pt. 1:4) and become a temple of the Holy Spirit (cf. 1 Cor. 3:16), God's friend (cf. Jn. 15:15) and adopted child (cf. 1 Jn. 3:1), and an heir of heaven (cf. Rom. 8:16-17). Sanctifying grace also makes us capable of meriting the heavenly reward for our good actions (cf. Rom. 2:6).

### 223. Why is sanctifying grace also called "habitual" grace?

Sanctifying grace is also called habitual grace because it permanently inheres in our soul. It is also called an infused habit.

### 224. Is sanctifying grace necessary for our salvation?

Sanctifying grace is necessary for our salvation because it alone makes us able to attain to the supernatural happiness of the beatific vision of God in heaven, which is beyond the capacity of all human nature.

### 225. What does it mean to be in the state of grace?

To be in the state of grace means to be in a state of friendship with God.

### 226. Can sanctifying grace be lost?

Yes, sanctifying grace can be lost, and it is lost by every mortal sin.

> Therefore let any one who thinks that he stands take heed lest he fall (1 Cor. 10:12).

### 227. Can sanctifying grace be recovered?

Yes, sanctifying grace can be recovered. The ordinary means of recovering grace is the Sacrament of Penance or Reconciliation.

### 228. Can sanctifying grace be increased?

Yes, sanctifying grace can be increased by good works, prayer, and devout reception of the sacraments, especially the Holy Eucharist.

## Other Divine Gifts

### 229. Together with sanctifying grace do we receive other supernatural gifts?

Yes, with sanctifying grace God infuses into our souls the virtues of faith, hope and charity, which make us capable of performing ordinary acts of Christian virtue. He also infuses the gifts of the

Holy Spirit, which enable us to respond easily and joyfully to actual grace and even to perform heroic acts of virtue.

### 230. Which are the gifts of the Holy Spirit?

The gifts of the Holy Spirit are seven: wisdom, understanding, counsel, fortitude, knowledge, piety, and fear of the Lord.

## Actual Grace

### 231. What is actual grace?

Actual grace is a divine enlightenment of our mind and a divine strengthening of our will to enable us to avoid evil and do what is pleasing to God.

> I will instruct you and teach you
>     the way you should go;
>         I will counsel you with my eye upon you
> (Ps. 32:8).

> Now may the God of peace...equip you with everything good that you may do his will, working in you that which is pleasing in his sight... (Heb. 13:20-21).

### 232. Is actual grace necessary?

Actual grace is absolutely necessary in order to perform actions that are pleasing to God and which lead toward heaven.

> ...for God is at work in you, both to will and to work for his good pleasure (Phil. 2:13).

> "...apart from me you can do nothing" (Jn. 15:5).

**233. Does God give sufficient grace to all?**
Yes, God gives sufficient grace to all, for their salvation. God gives everyone enough grace to keep His Commandments, and to sinners He gives enough grace to be converted.

> "For my yoke is easy, and my burden is light" (Mt. 11:30).

> "As I live, says the Lord God, I have no pleasure in the death of the wicked, but that the wicked turn from his way and live..." (Ez. 33:11).

**234. Can God's grace be resisted?**
God's grace can be resisted because we have free will and God will never force us to accept His help.

**235. Is there a way we can dispose ourselves to respond positively to actual grace?**
We can dispose ourselves to respond positively to actual grace by prayer.

# THE SACRAMENTS IN GENERAL

## Grace-giving Signs

**236. What is a sacrament?**
A sacrament is an external sign instituted by Christ through which He gives us His grace.

DSP

**Each of the seven sacraments
gives grace to the recipient.**

**237. How many sacraments are there?**
There are seven sacraments: Baptism, Confirmation, Holy Eucharist, Penance or Reconciliation, Anointing of the Sick, Holy Orders and Matrimony.

**238. Were all seven sacraments instituted by Jesus Christ?**
Yes, all seven sacraments were instituted by Jesus Christ before His return to His Father.

**239. Do all the sacraments give grace?**
Because of the merits of Jesus' passion and death, all the sacraments give grace if they are received with the right dispositions.

> "Just as the Father who has life sent me
> and I have life because of the Father,
> so the man who feeds on me
> will have life because of me"
> (Jn. 6:57 NAB).

**240. Which graces do the sacraments give?**
The sacraments give or increase sanctifying grace; they also give sacramental grace.

**241. What is sacramental grace?**
Sacramental grace is the special grace proper to a particular sacrament which gives us the right to those actual graces that will help us attain that sacrament's purpose.

## Kinds of Sacraments

**242. How may the sacraments be grouped?**
The sacraments may be grouped as follows: initiation (3), reconciliation (2), vocation (2).

**243. Which are the sacraments of initiation?**
Baptism, Confirmation and Eucharist are the sacraments of initiation, or of beginning in the Christian life.

**244. Which are the sacraments of reconciliation?**
Penance (Reconciliation) and the Anointing of the Sick are the sacraments of reconciliation or peacemaking.

**245. Which are the sacraments of vocation?**
Holy Orders and Matrimony are the sacraments of vocation or of calling to a particular state in life.

**246. Can some sacraments be received only once?**
Baptism, Confirmation and Holy Orders can be received only once because they give the soul a spiritual quality, called a character, which lasts forever.

## Elements of a Sacrament

**247. What constitutes a true sacrament?**
Two elements are needed to constitute a true sacrament: matter and form.

**248. What is meant by "matter"?**
"Matter" means some sensible, concrete thing or action, such as anointing with oil, pouring of water, etc.

**249. What is meant by "form"?**
"Form" means the essential words or sign used by the minister—for example, "I absolve you from your sins."

**250. Must the matter and form be united?**
Yes, the matter must be performed and the form must be used at the same time and by the same minister.

**251. What is meant by the "minister" of a sacrament?**
The minister of a sacrament is a person who has received from Jesus the power to act for Him in giving that particular sacrament.

**252. Does the effectiveness of a sacrament depend on the holiness of the minister?**
The effectiveness of a sacrament does not depend on the holiness of the minister. Instead, the measure of the grace that Jesus distributes to us is limited only by our dispositions.

A. Pisano

"Let the children come to me, and
do not hinder them; for to such belongs
the kingdom of heaven" (Mt. 19:14).

## Reception of the Sacraments

### 253. What dispositions should we have in receiving the sacraments?

We should especially receive the sacraments with faith and love, but also with trust in God's mercy and sorrow for our sins.

### 254. Is the state of grace necessary for the reception of the sacraments?

The state of grace is necessary for the reception of the majority of the sacraments, namely: Confirmation, Holy Eucharist, Holy Orders, Matrimony and normally the Anointing of the Sick.

## BAPTISM

### The First Sacrament

### 255. What is Baptism?

Baptism is the sacrament which removes original sin and all personal sins. It makes us children of God, brothers and sisters of Jesus Christ, heirs of heaven and members of the Church, with a right to receive the other sacraments.

### 256. Did Jesus make Baptism obligatory?

Jesus made Baptism obligatory when He said to His Apostles: "Go into all the world and preach the gospel to the whole creation. He who believes and is baptized will be saved; but he who does not believe will be condemned" (Mk. 16:15-16).

### 257. Does Baptism remove all sin?

Baptism removes original sin for everyone, and actual sin for adults who are sorry, as well as the punishment due to sin.

> Let us draw near in utter sincerity and absolute confidence, our hearts sprinkled clean from the evil which lay on our conscience and our bodies washed in pure water (Heb. 10:22 NAB).

### 258. What does the character of Baptism do for us?

The character or seal of Baptism confers on us a permanent relationship with Christ which will identify us as Christians and Catholics in this life and into eternity.

### 259. Who usually baptizes?

The ordinary minister of Baptism is a priest or deacon.

## Emergency Baptism

### 260. In case of emergency, who can baptize?

In case of emergency, anyone, even a non-Christian, may validly baptize.

### 261. How is emergency or private Baptism given?

The person baptizing must:

—want to do what the Church intends;

—pour ordinary water on the head three times, so that it flows on the skin;

—say at the same time: "I baptize you in the name of the Father and of the Son and of the Holy Spirit."

### 262. If the baptized person survives, is the baptism to be repeated?

No, if the baptized person survives, the baptism is not to be repeated, but the ceremonies surrounding Baptism are to be performed in church by a priest or deacon.

## Importance of Baptism

### 263. Is Baptism necessary for salvation?

Baptism is necessary for salvation because Jesus said: "Unless one is born of water and the Spirit, he cannot enter the kingdom of God" (Jn. 3:5).

### 264. Can Baptism be repeated and do the "born again Christians" really receive a "new baptism"?

There is no validity in a second baptism. This sacrament imprints a lasting character on the soul of the baptized, a consecration to Christ which will last forever. Thus, once one is baptized, he or she is a Christian forever.

### 265. Should infants be baptized?

Infants should be baptized within the first weeks after birth. If a child is in danger of death, it is to be baptized without delay. If an infant dies without Baptism, that is, departs from this life with original sin, his destiny is left to God's goodness, but many hold that such an infant goes to limbo. The Church has made no declaration on the subject of limbo.

### 266. What is limbo?

St. Thomas teaches that limbo is a place of natural happiness, without the vision of God.

### 267. Can an adult who dies without Baptism be saved?

An adult who dies unbaptized because he does not know about Baptism or its importance can be saved if during his life he tried to do good and avoid evil. This is called "baptism of desire." The martyrdom of such a person for the Faith is called "baptism of blood."

## Godparents

### 268. What are the responsibilities of godparents?

Godparents must see to it that their godchildren are raised as good Catholics if this is not done by the parents. However, because of their natural relationship, parents are to remember that they have a greater role than the godparents in the Baptism of their infants. Therefore, it is very important for them to prepare well for this great event and to be present at the celebration of Baptism.

### 269. Whom should parents choose as godparents?

Parents should choose as godparents only those who know and live their Catholic Faith.

## Baptismal Promises and Name

### 270. What did our parents and godparents promise for us in Baptism?

In Baptism, our parents and godparents promised for us that we would reject Satan and everything contrary to the law of God and live according to the teachings and examples of Jesus Christ.

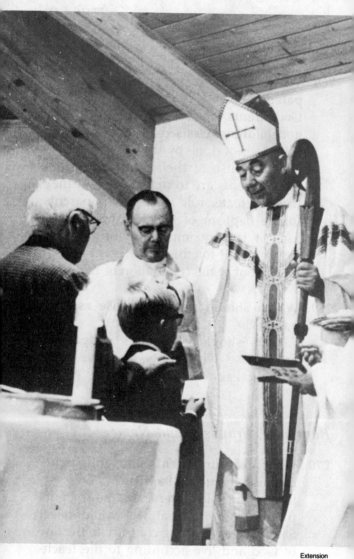

Extension

# The Holy Spirit strengthens us.

271. **Why are the baptismal promises important?**

The baptismal promises are important because they guide us on the road to eternal life.

272. **Why do we receive a saint's name in Baptism?**

We receive a saint's name in Baptism so that we may imitate the virtues of our patron saint and have a protector in heaven.

## CONFIRMATION

### Sacrament of Witness

273. **What is Confirmation?**

Confirmation is the sacrament instituted by Jesus Christ to give us the Holy Spirit in a special way. It joins us more closely to Jesus' Church and gives a special strength to enable us to share and defend our Faith, both by words and by deeds, as true witnesses of Christ.

> "He who believes in me, as the scripture has said, 'Out of his heart shall flow rivers of living water.'" Now this he said about the Spirit, which those who believed in him were to receive (Jn. 7:38-39).

274. **What else does Confirmation do for us?**

Confirmation increases in our soul sanctifying grace, the supernatural virtues and the gifts of the Holy Spirit. It confers the indelible character of a witness to Christ and a special sacramental grace that enables us to be ever courageous in professing our Faith.

### 275. How do we know that Jesus instituted the Sacrament of Confirmation?

We know that Jesus instituted the Sacrament of Confirmation from the historical books of the New Testament (cf. Acts 8:14-17; 19:6).

## Rite of Confirmation

### 276. Who is the minister of Confirmation?

The bishop is the ordinary minister of Confirmation, but priests, too, may confirm in case of emergency or when they have permission to do so.

### 277. How is Confirmation given?

Confirmation is given by tracing a cross on the person's forehead with blessed oil, called chrism, while saying: "Be sealed with the gift of the Holy Spirit."

### 278. What is holy chrism?

Holy chrism is a mixture of olive oil and balsam blessed by the bishop on Holy Thursday usually.

## 279. Why is a cross traced on the person's forehead?

A cross is traced on the person's forehead as a symbol of the Faith that the person who is confirmed must live and profess even when it is difficult to do so.

## *Importance of Confirmation*

## 280. Who can receive Confirmation?

Any baptized person who was never confirmed can receive Confirmation.

## 281. How should one prepare for Confirmation?

One should prepare for Confirmation by being in the state of grace and knowing the main truths and duties of the Catholic Faith.

## 282. Is Confirmation valid if one receives it in mortal sin?

Should Confirmation be received in mortal sin, it is valid, but the person sins grievously and does not receive the special graces of this sacrament until he reacquires the state of grace through a good confession.

## 283. Who should be confirmed?

Even though Confirmation is not absolutely necessary for salvation, every Catholic should be confirmed, because

"This is my body, which will be given for you" (Lk. 22:19).

this sacrament makes us strong in our Faith and prepares us to carry out our baptismal obligation of sharing the Faith with others.

284. **After Confirmation, are we still obliged to study our Catholic Faith?**
After Confirmation we are still obliged to study our Catholic Faith with even greater care so that we will understand and live it ever better and be able to explain it to others.

> Always be prepared to make a defense to any one who calls you to account for the hope that is in you, yet do it with gentleness and reverence (1 Pt. 3:15).

## Confirmation Sponsor

285. **Who should be chosen as a sponsor for Confirmation?**
A practicing Catholic should be chosen as a sponsor for Confirmation, because of the sponsor's responsibility for the Christian education of the candidate.

# HOLY EUCHARIST

## The Real Presence

286. **What is the Holy Eucharist?**
The Holy Eucharist is that sacrament in which Jesus Christ, under the forms of bread and wine, is truly present in

His Body and Blood, in order to offer Himself to the heavenly Father for our salvation and give Himself to us as nourishment for our souls.

### 287. When did Jesus institute the Holy Eucharist?

Jesus Christ instituted the Holy Eucharist at the Last Supper, the night before His death on the cross; this was the very first Mass (cf. Mt. 26:26-28).

### 288. How did Jesus Christ institute the Holy Eucharist?

Jesus Christ instituted the Holy Eucharist in this way: "He took some bread, and when he had given thanks, broke it and gave it to them saying, 'This is my body which will be given for you; do this as a memorial of me.' He did the same with the cup after supper, and said, 'This cup is the new covenant in my blood which will be poured out for you'" (Lk. 22:19-20 JB).

### 289. When Jesus said, "This is my body" and "This is my blood," what happened to the bread and wine?

When Jesus said "This is my body," the entire substance of the bread was changed into His real Body; and when He said "This is my blood," the entire substance of the wine was changed into His real Blood.

"For my flesh is food indeed, and my blood is drink indeed" (Jn. 6:55).

**290. Are the Body and Blood of Jesus Christ really present in the Holy Eucharist?**
Yes, the Body and Blood of Jesus Christ are really present in the Holy Eucharist (cf. Mt. 26:26-28; Mk. 14:22-24; Lk. 22:15-20; 1 Cor. 11:23-25).

## Effecting Christ's Real Presence

**291. How does Jesus become present in the Holy Eucharist?**
Jesus becomes present in the Holy Eucharist by a change called transubstantiation.

**292. What is transubstantiation?**
Transubstantiation is the change of the entire substance of the bread and the entire substance of the wine into the real Body and Blood of Jesus Christ.

## Total Presence

**293. Is the whole Christ truly present in the Holy Eucharist after the transubstantiation?**
Yes, the whole Christ in His body, blood, soul and divinity—true God and true man—is truly present after the transubstantiation.

294. **Is the whole Christ present in each particle of the consecrated host and in each drop of the consecrated wine?**
Yes, the whole Christ is present in each particle of the consecrated host and each drop of the consecrated wine.

295. **What remains of the bread and wine after Jesus changes them into His Body and Blood?**
After Jesus changes the bread and wine into His Body and Blood, only the appearances (color, weight, odor, taste, shape) of bread and wine remain.

296. **Is the Real Presence of Christ in the Holy Eucharist a mystery of faith?**
Yes, the Real Presence of Christ in the Holy Eucharist is a mystery of faith.

297. **How is Jesus able to change bread and wine into His Body and Blood?**
Jesus is able to change bread and wine into His Body and Blood because He is God and can do all things.

298. **Why does Jesus give us His own Body and Blood in the Eucharist?**
Jesus gives us His Body and Blood in this sacrament: to be offered as a sacrifice,

perpetually renewing His sacrifice of the cross; to be received in Holy Communion; and, to be present in our churches to show His love and be adored by us.

## *The Mass, or Eucharistic Celebration*

### 299. What is the Mass?

The Mass, or Eucharistic Celebration, is at one and the same time: the sacrifice of the cross made present on our altars; a memorial of Jesus' saving death, resurrection and ascension; a sacred banquet in which Christ is received.

### 300. Who can celebrate Mass?

Only a validly ordained priest can celebrate a valid Mass, because only a validly ordained priest has the power of consecration—that is, of changing the bread and wine into the Body and Blood of Jesus Christ.

### 301. When did Jesus give priests the power of celebrating the Sacrifice of the Mass?

Jesus gave priests the power of celebrating the Sacrifice of the Mass at the Last Supper, when He said to His Apostles: "Do this in commemoration of me" (Lk. 22:19; cf. 1 Cor. 11:24).

## 302. When does the change of bread and wine into the Body and Blood of Jesus Christ take place?

The change of bread and wine into the Body and Blood of Jesus Christ takes place at the consecration of the Sacrifice of the Mass, when the priest repeats the words of Christ, "This is my body" and "This is my blood."

## The Mass: a Sacrifice

## 303. What is a sacrifice?

A sacrifice is the offering of a victim to God by a priest, who immolates it in some way to show that all things, and also the persons making the offering, belong to God, the Creator.

## 304. Is the Mass a true sacrifice?

The Mass is a true sacrifice in which Jesus Christ offers Himself to the Father through the priest, as a victim, under the appearances of bread and wine.

> For from the rising of the sun to its setting my name is great among the nations, and in every place incense is offered to my name, and a pure offering; for my name is great among the nations, says the Lord of hosts (Mal. 1:11).

305. **Is the Mass the same sacrifice as that of the cross?**

Yes, the Mass is the same sacrifice as that of the cross, because in the Mass Jesus' sacrifice on the cross is made present, its memory is celebrated and its saving power is applied for the forgiveness of the sins which we daily commit.

306. **In which ways is the Sacrifice of the Mass the same as the sacrifice of the cross?**

In the Sacrifice of the Mass and in the sacrifice of the cross the Victim and Priest are the same: Jesus Christ, who now offers Himself to the Father through the ministry of His priests.

307. **How does the Sacrifice of the Mass differ from the sacrifice of the cross?**

On the cross Jesus offered Himself to the Father in a bloody manner by a real separation of His Body and Blood; in the Holy Mass Jesus offers Himself in an unbloody manner, because He is risen and can die no more.

308. **At what point in the Mass does Jesus offer Himself to His heavenly Father as a victim for our salvation?**

Jesus offers Himself to His heavenly Father as a victim for our salvation at the consecration of the Mass. The double consecration represents the mystical separation of Jesus' Body and Blood. Even the words express Jesus' sacrifice for our sins: "This is my body which will be given up for you.... This is the cup of my blood.... It will be shed for you and for all so that sins may be forgiven."

## Purpose and Effects of the Mass

**309. What is the purpose of the Sacrifice of the Mass?**

The purpose of the Sacrifice of the Mass is the same as that of the sacrifice of the cross: the glorification of the heavenly Father, whom we praise and thank for His benefits; expiation or reparation for our own sins and those of all mankind; appeal for the supernatural and natural favors that we need.

**310. Is the Mass to be offered to God alone?**

Yes, the Mass is to be offered to God alone, because of the infinite dignity of the Priest and Victim.

**311. What is meant by offering the Mass to commemorate saints?**

When the Church celebrates Masses to commemorate the saints, she does not offer the sacrifice to the saints, but to God alone, with the intention of thanking Him for the grace and glory given to them and also to appeal to Him through their intercession.

312. **Can the Sacrifice of the Mass be offered for the poor souls in purgatory?**
Yes, the Sacrifice of the Mass can be offered to God for the poor souls in purgatory, because in the Mass the forgiveness of sins and of the punishment due to sin is applied not only for the living but also for the dead.

> "...for this is my blood of the covenant, which is poured out for many for the forgiveness of sins" (Mt. 26:28).

> For every high priest chosen from among men is appointed to act on behalf of men in relation to God, to offer gifts and sacrifices for sins (Heb. 5:1).

313. **Which are the effects of the Sacrifice of the Mass for us personally?**
The Sacrifice of the Mass remits our venial sins and the temporal punishment still due to forgiven sins; it increases sanctifying grace in our souls, together with the infused virtues and the gifts of the Holy Spirit. The Mass has an infinite value, but we receive its effects according to our dispositions.

### 314. How should we participate in Holy Mass?

We should participate in Holy Mass with attention, joining our prayers to those of the priest, with the same dispositions we would have had at the foot of the cross, because on the cross Jesus accomplished our redemption, and in the Mass He applies it to us.

## Which Bread and Wine?

### 315. In order for the Mass to be valid, what kind of bread must be used?

In order for the Mass to be valid, the bread used must be made of pure wheaten flour and water, with no admixture of milk, eggs, honey or other ingredients.

### 316. In order for the Mass to be valid, what kind of wine must be used?

In order for the Mass to be valid, the wine used must be natural grape wine. Ecclesiastical approval of the wine should be had.

## Parts of the Mass

### 317. How is the Mass divided?

The Mass is divided into two parts: the "Liturgy of the Word" and the "Liturgy of the Eucharist." In the first part Jesus speaks to us through the Bible; in the second part Jesus offers Himself to the Father for our salvation, as He did on the cross, and gives Himself to us in Holy Communion, to make us one with Him.

## The Liturgical Renewal

318. **In general, what was the liturgical renewal called for by Vatican II?**

Vatican II called for: greater awareness of the meaning of the Mass; more active and personal participation; a more vivid sense of community.

319. **Did the Second Vatican Council call for "less use of Latin" in the Mass or did it simply allow the use of the vernacular?**

Vatican II called for less use of Latin and more use of the vernacular in order that the majority of the faithful might better understand and profit from the spiritual riches of the Eucharistic Celebration.

## Holy Communion

320. **What is Holy Communion?**

Holy Communion is the receiving of the Body and Blood of Jesus Christ in the Sacrament of the Holy Eucharist, for the nourishment of our soul.

> Jesus said to them, "Truly, truly, I say to you, unless you eat the flesh of the Son of man and drink his blood, you have no life in you" (Jn. 6:53).

## 321. What is the chief fruit of Holy Communion?

The chief fruit of Holy Communion is an interior and most intimate union with Jesus Christ.

> "He who eats my flesh and drinks my blood abides in me, and I in him" (Jn. 6:56).

## 322. Does Holy Communion also produce brotherly unity?

Holy Communion also produces brotherly unity, because in Communion we receive Jesus Christ, who is the Head of the Mystical Body. From this follows the unity of the faithful with one another because we are members of the Mystical Body.

> Because there is one bread, we who are many are one body, for we all partake of the one bread (1 Cor. 10:17).

## 323. Which are other fruits of Holy Communion?

Holy Communion increases sanctifying grace, the virtues of faith, hope and love associated with it, and the gifts of the Holy Spirit. It remits venial sins and the temporal punishment due to sin. It weakens concupiscence, reinforces the power of the will, preserves one from falling into mortal sin, and also gives rise to a joyful acceptance of the duties and sacrifices demanded by Christian life.

324. **What did Jesus mean when He said: "he who eats my flesh and drinks my blood has eternal life, and I will raise him up at the last day"? (Jn. 6:54)**

With these words Jesus meant to tell us that Holy Communion is a pledge of heavenly bliss and of the future resurrection of the body.

325. **Which are the necessary conditions for receiving Holy Communion worthily?**

To receive Holy Communion worthily, there are two necessary conditions: to be in the state of grace and to have the right intention.

326. **What does it mean to be in the state of grace?**

To be in the state of grace means to be free from mortal sin.

> Let a man examine himself, and so eat of the bread and drink of the cup (1 Cor. 11:28).

327. **If a person knows that he is in the state of mortal sin and receives Holy Communion, does he still receive Jesus?**

A person who receives Holy Communion, knowing that he is in the state of mortal sin, does receive Jesus, but does not receive His grace, and commits the mortal sin of sacrilege.

### 328. What does it mean to have the right intention?

To have the right intention means to receive Holy Communion in order to show God our love and be more united with Him. We are to avoid harboring other intentions, such as human respect or vanity.

### 329. What other good dispositions should we have when preparing for Holy Communion?

We are to be free, if possible, from fully deliberate venial sins and make acts of faith, hope, love, sorrow and desire.

### 330. What fast are we to observe before receiving Holy Communion?

We are not to have taken any food or beverages (except water) for one hour before receiving. (Those who are ill or elderly, even if not confined to bed, may reduce this time to fifteen minutes whenever it would be difficult for them to fast for an hour. They may take medicines at any time.)

### 331. Should we receive Communion kneeling or standing?

We may receive Holy Communion either kneeling or standing. If we receive standing, we should make a sign of reverence before receiving.

### 332. After receiving Holy Communion, what should we do?

After receiving Holy Communion we should adore Jesus present in us, thank Him for coming, renew our love and desire to do His will, and ask Him to bless us and others.

### 333. How can we derive the greatest spiritual benefits from Holy Communion?

Since the measure of grace received in Holy Communion is in proportion to our personal dispositions, we should make a good preparation and a good thanksgiving.

### 334. When are we obliged to receive Holy Communion?

We are obliged to receive Holy Communion at least once a year (during the Easter time) and when in danger of death, as Viaticum.

> "...he who eats my flesh and drinks my blood has eternal life, and I will raise him up at the last day" (Jn. 6:54).

### 335. Is it good to receive Holy Communion frequently?

We should receive Holy Communion frequently, even daily, to obtain the strength we need to live a good Christian life and grow continually in God's grace.

### 336. Who should receive Holy Communion?

Since Jesus tells us that the possession of eternal life will depend on the receiving of His Body and Blood (cf. Jn. 6:54), the reception of Holy Communion is necessary for adults. This obligation begins when the person reaches the use of reason—that is, approximately in the seventh year.

### 337. Why is the reception of Holy Communion necessary for adults?

The reception of Holy Communion is necessary for adults because Jesus gave us Himself in the Holy Eucharist as nourishment for our souls. Therefore, without Communion, the supernatural life—that is, the state of grace—cannot be permanently preserved.

> "Truly, truly, I say to you, unless you eat the flesh of the Son of man and drink his blood, you have no life in you" (Jn. 6:53).

**338. Are the faithful permitted to receive Holy Communion under both kinds?**

Yes, the faithful are permitted to receive Holy Communion under both kinds, only on certain occasions. But they are not obliged to do so. The Lord is present, whole and entire, under both species.

## Eucharistic Devotion

**339. Does the Real Presence of Jesus in the consecrated host continue after Mass?**

Yes, the Real Presence of Jesus in the consecrated host continues after Mass.

**340. How can we show our Lord how much we appreciate His continual Presence in the tabernacle?**

We can show our Lord how much we appreciate His continual Presence in the tabernacle by making frequent visits to Him in the Blessed Sacrament and by taking part in parish devotions which especially honor the Holy Eucharist, such as Benediction of the Blessed Sacrament and the Forty Hours Devotion.

# PENANCE OR RECONCILIATION

**341. What is the Sacrament of Penance or Reconciliation?**

Penance or Reconciliation is the sacrament, instituted by Christ, in which,

"Father, I have sinned against God
and against you" (Lk. 15:21).

through the merits of His passion and death, He forgives sins committed after Baptism when a penitent confesses them and receives absolution by the priest.

**342. Do the Gospels tell us about Jesus' institution of this sacrament?**

Yes, the Gospels tell us about Jesus' institution of this sacrament. In Matthew 16:19 and 18:18 the power of binding and loosing (retaining and forgiving) was promised first to Peter and then to the other Apostles. The actual institution of Penance is related in John 20:22-23: "Receive the Holy Spirit. If you forgive the sins of any, they are forgiven; if you retain the sins of any, they are retained."

**343. Does the priest actually forgive our sins?**

Yes, the priest actually forgives our sins, as can be seen from John 20:23. He does so in Jesus' name and by Jesus' power.

**344. Why do we have to confess our sins to the priest in order to obtain forgiveness?**

We must confess our sins to the priest because, in order to exercise the power that Jesus gave him (cf. Jn. 20:23) the priest has to know what our sins are and whether we are sorry and intend to avoid them and their near occasions in the future.

### 345. What constitutes the sign of the Sacrament of Penance?

The matter consists of the penitent's sins and the acts required of the penitent, which are, sorrow, confession—which is the telling of our sins to the confessor—and the acceptance of the penance. The form consists of the words of the priest: "God, the Father of mercies, through the death and resurrection of his Son has reconciled the world to himself and sent the Holy Spirit among us for the forgiveness of sins; through the ministry of his Church may God give you pardon and peace, and I absolve you from your sins in the name of the Father and of the Son and of the Holy Spirit."

### 346. Who must receive Penance or Reconciliation?

Penance or Reconciliation must be received by anyone who has committed a mortal sin after Baptism.

### 347. What does the Sacrament of Penance do for us?

If well received, the Sacrament of Penance:

—restores or increases sanctifying grace;

—forgives our sins;

—removes the eternal punishment for

serious sin and at least part of the temporal punishment;

—helps us to avoid future sins;

—and restores the merits that had been lost by mortal sin.

> We beseech you on behalf of Christ, be reconciled to God. For our sake he made him to be sin who knew no sin, so that in him we might become the righteousness of God (2 Cor. 5:20-21).

### 348. What is required to make a good confession?

To make a good confession, we should examine our conscience well, be truly sorry for our sins, resolve not to sin again, tell our sins to the priest, and do the penance he gives us.

> "Have I any pleasure in the death of the wicked, says the Lord God, and not rather that he should turn from his way and live?" (Ez. 18:23)

### 349. What does "examination of conscience" mean?

"Examination of conscience" means a deliberate recalling of sins, especially mortal sins, that have been committed since the last good confession.

### 350. How can we make a good examination of conscience?

To make a good examination of conscience, we should first ask God's help, and then examine ourselves on the commandments of God, the laws of the Church, and the special duties of our state in life.

> Why should a living man complain,
>    a man, about the punishment of his sins?
> Let us test and examine our ways, and
>    return to the Lord!
> Let us lift up our hearts and hands to God
>    in heaven (Lam. 3:39-41).

### 351. What is contrition?

Contrition is true sorrow for sin and hatred for anything that offends God, joined to a firm resolution to sin no more.

### 352. When is our sorrow true contrition?

Our sorrow is true contrition when it leads us to hate sin as the greatest evil—an offense to God—and when it extends to every mortal sin not yet forgiven.

> "If my people who are called by my name humble themselves, and pray and seek my face, and turn from their wicked ways, then I will hear from heaven, and will forgive their sin and heal their land" (2 Chr. 7:14).

### 353. Is it necessary to have *true contrition* for mortal sin?

It is necessary to have true contrition for every mortal sin because there is no greater evil than sin, which greatly offends God, robs us of grace, and makes us deserving of hell.

> The sacrifice acceptable to God is a broken spirit;
>> a broken and contrite heart, O God, you will not despise (Ps. 51:17).

### 354. How many kinds of contrition are there?

There are two kinds of true contrition: perfect and imperfect.

### 355. What is perfect contrition?

Perfect contrition is sorrow for sin because it offends God, who is infinitely good and loving, and deserves all our love in return.

> Against you, you only, have I sinned,
>> and done that which is evil in your sight,
> so that you are justified in your sentence
>> and blameless in your judgment
>>> (Ps. 51:4).

### 356. What is imperfect contrition?

Imperfect contrition is sorrow for sin for motives which are less pure, yet still supernatural, for example: because we fear God's punishments, or because sins are hateful in themselves.

### 357. What kind of contrition must we have to receive the Sacrament of Penance well?

To receive the Sacrament of Penance well, we must have at least imperfect contrition, but perfect contrition is better and more pleasing to God, who will give it to us if we ask Him.

**358. Can a person in mortal sin regain sanctifying grace before going to confession?**
A person in mortal sin can regain sanctifying grace before going to confession by making an act of perfect contrition with the resolution of going to confession. But in the meantime he cannot go to Communion.

**359. Should we also be sorry for all our venial sins?**
We should also be sorry for all our venial sins, because every sin is an offense against the all-good, all-loving God.

**360. Why else should we be sorry for venial sins?**
We should also be sorry for venial sin because it makes us deserving of punishment, and weakens our resistance to mortal sin.

**361. What does the firm decision to sin no more mean?**
The firm decision to sin no more means we are determined to avoid sin and, as far as possible, even near occasions of sin.

"Watch and pray that you may not enter into temptation; the spirit indeed is willing, but the flesh is weak" (Mk. 14:38).

Flee from sin as from a snake;
　　for if you approach sin, it will bite you
　　(Sir. 21:2).

### 362. When should we express our contrition to God?

The rite of Penance makes provision for an act of contrition to be said in the confessional. However, it is well also to express our contrition to God before making our confession.

### 363. What is confession?

Confession is the actual telling of our sins to an authorized priest to obtain God's forgiveness through the priest's absolution.

### 364. How should we go to confession?

When we enter the confessional, we should make the Sign of the Cross and listen to the passage of Scripture read or quoted by the priest. Then we tell the priest our state in life (married, single, religious), mention the length of time since our last confession, and say our sins as simply and truthfully as we can, especially each and every mortal sin, specifying the number of times committed and whatever circumstances alter the nature of the sin. After confession we accept the penance imposed on us and recite an act of contrition.

### 365. Must we confess every sin?

We must confess every mortal sin which has never been confessed. We are not obliged to confess every venial sin, although it is better to do so.

### 366. Will God forgive any sin?

God will forgive any sin, mortal or venial, if we are sincerely sorry for it.

> God, who is rich in mercy, out of the great love with which he loved us, even when we were dead through our trespasses, made us alive together with Christ (by grace you have been saved) (Eph. 2:4-5).

### 367. Should shame or fear ever keep us from confessing a mortal sin?

Shame or fear should never keep us from confessing a mortal sin because the priest represents the merciful Christ, and is bound by the seal of confession never to reveal any sin.

> For we have not a high priest who is unable to sympathize with our weaknesses, but one who in every respect has been tempted as we are, yet without sinning. Let us then with confidence draw near to the throne of grace, that we may receive mercy and find grace to help in time of need (Heb. 4:15-16).

### 368. What if someone deliberately omits confessing a mortal sin?

If someone deliberately omits confessing a mortal sin, the other sins that he or she confesses are not forgiven and the mortal sin of sacrilege is committed.

> He who conceals his transgressions will not prosper,
>> but he who confesses and forsakes them will obtain mercy (Prv. 28:13).

### 369. What must a person do who has knowingly concealed a mortal sin in confession?

A person who has knowingly concealed a mortal sin in confession must confess that he or she has made a bad confession, tell the sin concealed, the sacraments received since that time, and confess all the other mortal sins committed since his or her last good confession.

### 370. What should we do if we forget to confess a mortal sin?

If we forget to confess a mortal sin, we may receive Holy Communion, since we made a good confession and God forgave the sin, but we are obliged to confess that sin the next time we go to confession.

**371. Is it important to confess venial sins?**
It is important to confess venial sins, for such sins weaken us spiritually, and the Sacrament of Penance renews our strength.

**372. Of what must we be careful in confessing venial sins only?**
In confessing venial sins only, we must be careful to have sorrow for at least one of them; otherwise, the confession will be invalid.

**373. Why do persons sometimes confess one or more sins of their past life?**
Persons sometimes confess one or more sins of their past life in order to obtain the grace not to fall again. As always, to be valid this confession must include sorrow.

**374. What is to be said of the frequent confession of venial sins?**
The frequent confession of venial sins is an excellent means of spiritual progress. By it we grow in self-knowledge, humility and self-control; correct our bad habits; purify our conscience; strengthen our will; keep fervent; grow in grace.

### 375. How may we conclude the confession of our sins?

We may conclude the confession of our sins by saying: "I am sorry for these and for all the sins of my past life, especially...," and then add a sin previously confessed for which we are especially sorry.

### 376. What should we do after we tell our sins to the priest?

After we tell our sins to the priest we should sincerely answer any questions he may ask us, seek advice if we need to, listen to the priest's spiritual instruction, and accept the penance he gives.

> For the lips of a priest should guard knowledge, and men should seek instruction from his mouth, for he is the messenger of the Lord of hosts (Mal. 2:7).

### 377. Why do we receive a penance after confession?

We receive a penance after confession in order to make some satisfaction to God for our sins, receive His help, and lessen the punishment we deserve because of our sins.

### 378. What should we do before the priest gives us absolution?

Before the priest gives us absolution, we should say a fervent act of contrition.

### 379. May a priest refuse to give absolution?

A priest may refuse to give absolution if the penitent shows no signs of sorrow for the mortal sins he has confessed or gives no indication that he intends to avoid those sins or their occasions in the future.

## Satisfaction for Sin

### 380. What should we do after the confession?

After the confession we should thank God for the sacrament we have received, ask our Lord to make up for any imperfections in our confession, and do our penance with love and devotion.

### 381. Does the Sacrament of Penance remove all punishment due to sin?

If the Sacrament of Penance is well received, it always removes the eternal punishment of hell merited for mortal sin, but it does not always remove all temporal punishment.

### 382. Why is temporal punishment required by God?

God requires temporal, or temporary, punishment for sin because He is all-just and wants to teach us how evil sin is and to caution us to avoid it.

> "Behold, happy is the man whom God
>     reproves;
>     therefore despise not the chastening of
>         the Almighty.
> For he wounds, but he binds up;
>     he smites, but his hands heal"

(Jb. 5:17-18).

### 383. How can we satisfy the debt of temporal punishment?

We can satisfy the debt of temporal punishment either in purgatory or during this life with penance, the Mass, prayer, fasting, almsgiving, indulgences, the works of mercy, and the patient acceptance of trials and sufferings.

## Communal Celebration

### 384. What is a communal celebration of Penance?

A communal celebration of Penance consists of three acts: 1) communal penitential service; 2) individual confession and individual absolution; and 3) communal act of thanksgiving. Such a celebration is recommended when possible, because it shows even exteriorly that Penance reconciles us to God and to the Church.

## General Absolution

**385. What is general absolution and when may it be given?**

General absolution is a collective absolution. It may be given when individual confession and absolution are physically or morally impossible. Decisions as to when such absolution is to be permitted are left to the bishops.

**386. When general absolution is given, what must a person do in order to receive it validly?**

To validly receive general absolution a person must: 1) be truly sorry for his or her sins; 2) intend to tell these sins in the next confession if they were mortal; 3) resolve to avoid future sin.

## First Penance

**387. When should children begin to go to confession?**

Children should begin to go to confession when they reach the age of reason, which is usually about seven years old.

**388. Should first Penance precede first Communion?**

Yes, first Penance should precede first Communion. This is a directive of the

Church, given so that children may early form the habit of receiving this sacrament of spiritual growth and of fortification against temptation.

## Indulgences

**389. What is an indulgence?**
An indulgence is the remission, or removal—granted by the Church—of some or all of the temporal punishment due to our forgiven sins.

**390. What is a plenary indulgence?**
A plenary indulgence is an indulgence that removes all the temporal punishment we deserve because of our sins.

**391. What is a partial indulgence?**
A partial indulgence is an indulgence that removes only part of the temporal punishment we deserve because of our sins.

**392. How can the Church remove temporal punishment through indulgences?**
The Church can remove temporal punishment through indulgences by applying to us part of the superabundant merits of Jesus, of the Blessed Virgin Mary and the saints.

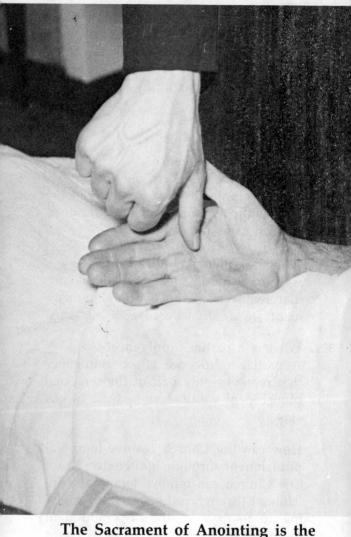

The Sacrament of Anointing is the continuation of Jesus' mission of bodily and spiritual healing.

393. **What is meant by the superabundant merits of Jesus, the Blessed Virgin Mary and the saints?**

By the superabundant merits of Jesus, the Blessed Virgin Mary and the saints is meant that during their lives they gained far greater merits than they themselves needed; these the Church applies to other members of the Mystical Body of Christ.

394. **For whom and how can we gain an indulgence?**

We can gain an indulgence for ourselves or for the holy souls in purgatory by being in the state of grace, having the desire of gaining the indulgence, and performing the good acts required by the Church.

## ANOINTING OF THE SICK

395. **What is the Anointing of the Sick?**

The Anointing of the Sick is the sacrament instituted by Christ which gives spiritual health and sometimes physical strength to persons in danger of death from serious illness, injury, or old age.

> So they [the Apostles] went out and preached that men should repent. And they cast out many demons, and anointed with oil many that were sick and healed them (Mk. 6:12-13).

### 396. How do we know that Jesus instituted the Anointing of the Sick?

We know that Jesus Christ instituted the Anointing of the Sick from the New Testament letter of James: "Is any among you sick? Let him call for the elders of the church, and let them pray over him, anointing him with oil in the name of the Lord; and the prayer of faith will save the sick man, and the Lord will raise him up; and if he has committed sins, he will be forgiven" (Jas. 5:14-15).

### 397. What does the Anointing of the Sick do for us?

The Anointing of the Sick increases sanctifying grace, makes suffering more meaningful and bearable, gives the strength to resist temptations, removes venial sins, removes temporal punishment due to sin, increases confidence in God, and sometimes restores physical health, if this is for the good of the person's soul.

### 398. How is the Anointing of the Sick a sacrament of reconciliation?

The Anointing of the Sick is a sacrament of reconciliation especially in this: it removes venial sins and even removes mortal sins (when the person is unable to confess them, but has at least made an act of imperfect contrition).

### 399. Who can confer the Anointing of the Sick?

Only a priest can confer the Anointing of the Sick.

### 400. Who may receive the Anointing of the Sick?

Anyone may receive the Anointing of the Sick who has been baptized, has attained the use of reason and is in danger of death (not necessarily on the point of death) from sickness, old age, or injury. The Church also encourages the elderly to receive the Anointing even when there seems to be no immediate danger of death.

### 401. How should one prepare to receive the Anointing of the Sick?

If possible, one should prepare to receive the Anointing of the Sick by making a good confession, by making acts of faith, hope and love, and by being totally resigned to the will of God.

> My son, when you are sick do not be negligent,
> but pray to the Lord, and he will heal you.

> Give up your faults and direct your
>   hands aright,
>   and cleanse your heart from all sin
>   (Sir. 38:9-10).

### 402. What is the matter of this sacrament?

The remote matter is plant oil which has been blessed by the bishop or an authorized priest (or in an emergency by any priest). The proximate matter is the anointing itself.

### 403. How is the Anointing of the Sick conferred?

The Anointing of the Sick is conferred by anointing the forehead and the hands while saying the words of the form: "Through this holy anointing may the Lord in his love and mercy help you with the grace of the Holy Spirit," and, "May the Lord who frees you from sin save you and raise you up." To both of these brief prayers of the priest the sick person responds, "Amen."

### 404. May the anointing be administered to a person about to undergo surgery?

Yes, the anointing may be administered to a person about to undergo surgery, if the reason for this surgery is a serious illness.

**405. May a person be anointed more than once?**

Yes, a person may be anointed more than once if there is a worsening of his or her condition or if there has been a recovery followed by a relapse or a new illness.

**406. May this sacrament be conferred on a person who has lost consciousness?**

Yes, this sacrament may and should be conferred on an unconscious person in danger of death.

**407. When should a priest be called to give the Anointing of the Sick?**

A priest should be called to give the Anointing of the Sick when someone becomes seriously ill, even if there is no immediate danger of death, so that the sick person will still be in a condition to derive the greatest fruits from this sacrament.

**408. Should a priest be called if someone has died suddenly?**

Yes, a priest should be called if someone has died suddenly, because he can give absolution and the Anointing of the Sick conditionally for some time after apparent death, since it is not certain that the person has really died.

Felici

**By the Sacrament of Holy Orders, priests share in the ministry of salvation that Christ accomplished in the world.**

## HOLY ORDERS

**409. What is Holy Orders?**

Holy Orders is the sacrament, instituted by Christ, which gives men the grace and power to carry out the sacred duties of deacons, priests or bishops.

"Do this in remembrance of me" (Lk. 22:19).

**410. What is the matter of the Sacrament of Holy Orders?**

The matter of the orders of diaconate, priesthood, and episcopate is the imposition of hands alone.

**411. Who can administer the Sacrament of Holy Orders?**

Only a validly consecrated bishop can administer the Sacrament of Holy Orders.

**412. Are bishops superior to priests?**

Yes, bishops possess the fullness of the priesthood. They have preeminence in both the power of jurisdiction and the power of consecration—the power to ordain and confirm.

**413. Who may receive Holy Orders?**

A man may receive Holy Orders who is a good Catholic, has prepared himself by the necessary studies, has the intention of giving his life to the service of God, and has been accepted by the bishop, or by one's Superior in the case of a priest who is a religious.

**414. Why cannot women be ordained to the priesthood?**

In fidelity to the example of Jesus, the Church does not consider herself authorized to ordain women, since Jesus never ordained women, not even His own Mother, and the constant practice and tradition of the Church, from the earliest times, has been to ordain only men.

**415. What are the effects of Holy Orders?**

Holy Orders increases sanctifying grace, gives the sacramental grace needed for the sacred ministry, gives a lasting character to the soul which is a sharing in the priesthood of Christ and is the source of special supernatural powers.

> I remind you to rekindle the gift of God that is within you through the laying on of my hands; for God did not give us a spirit of timidity but a spirit of power and love and self-control (2 Tm. 1:6-7).

**416. Which are the chief supernatural powers of the priest?**

The priest has the special supernatural powers to change bread and wine into the Body and Blood of Christ in the Mass, and to forgive sins in the Sacrament of Penance.

**417. Why is it that priests do not marry?**
Priests of the Latin rite do not marry so that by observing celibacy for the sake of the kingdom of heaven they may serve Christ with an undivided heart, dedicate themselves more freely and completely to their priestly ministry, and become living signs of the world to come.

**418. Do some Catholic priests marry?**
Some priests of the Eastern rite Catholic Churches marry, in accord with their ancient traditions, which have the approval of Rome.

**419. Does the Church have the right to require priestly celibacy?**
The Church has the right to set up obligatory disciplinary norms which every seminarian studies; if the seminarian decides to become a priest, he freely and knowingly accepts the norm of celibacy.

**420. What is the role of the deacon?**
The role of the deacon is to serve the people by administering Baptism, giving Communion, blessing marriages in the name of the Church, bringing Viaticum to the dying, reading the Scriptures to the faithful, instructing and exhorting the people, presiding over prayer ser-

The rings—sign of love and fidelity

vices, administering sacramentals, officiating at funeral and burial services, and performing duties of charity and administration.

### 421. May deacons marry?

Deacons may not marry. A single man ordained to the diaconate is to observe celibacy. However, a man who is already married may be ordained to the diaconate.

### 422. How should we regard bishops and priests?

Bishops and priests should be respected and honored in a special way because they represent Christ and give us God's grace.

> With all your souls fear the Lord,
>   and honor his priests.
> With all your might love your Maker,
>   and do not forsake his ministers.
> Fear the Lord and honor the priest,
>   and give him his portion, as is commanded you (Sir. 7:29-31).

## MATRIMONY

### Christian Marriage

### 423. What is Matrimony?

Matrimony is the sacrament instituted by Christ through which a baptized man and a baptized woman are united for life in a lawful marriage and receive God's grace to fulfill their responsibilities.

> He answered, "Have you not read that he who made them from the beginning made them male and female, and said, 'For this reason a man shall leave his father and mother and be joined to his wife, and the two shall become one'? So they are no longer two but one. What therefore God has joined together, let no man put asunder" (Mt. 19:5-6).

### 424. What is the purpose of marriage?

The purpose of marriage is twofold: unity and procreation, or the giving of love and the giving of life. The spouses commit themselves to loving, lifelong service—to one another and to the children whom God will send them.

### 425. Does Christian marriage have yet another dimension?

When we speak of *Christian* marriage, another dimension must also be included: growth in holiness. The spouses help one another to become holier; moreover, children and parents reciprocally contribute to the sanctification of one another.

### 426. When is marriage a sacrament?

Marriage is a sacrament when validly contracted between two baptized persons.

**427. How do we know that the Sacrament of Matrimony was instituted by Jesus Christ?**

We know that the Sacrament of Matrimony was instituted by Jesus Christ: 1) because Jesus taught the indissolubility of marriage (cf. Mt. 19:6 above), and the fulfillment of this precept calls for supernatural help; 2) because St. Paul compares Christian marriage to the permanent union between Christ and His Church (cf. Eph. 5:22-33) and stresses its importance; 3) because early Christian writings refer to Christian marriage as something supernatural, which confers grace on those who receive it; 4) because the Church has defined Matrimony as one of the seven sacraments instituted by Jesus Christ. The Fathers of the Church taught that Jesus sanctified marriage by His presence at the marriage of Cana (cf. Jn. 2:1-11).

**428. Why is marriage spoken of as a covenant?**

Marriage is spoken of as a covenant because it is a lifelong commitment. St. Paul tells us that Christian marriage is a sacred sign that reflects the lasting covenant which unites Christ to His Church: "'For this reason a man shall leave his father and mother and be joined to his wife, and the two shall become one.' This is a great mystery, and I mean in reference to Christ and the church..." (Eph. 5:31-32).

### 429. How is Matrimony conferred?

Matrimony is conferred when a baptized man and a baptized woman express their mutual consent under conditions established or permitted by the Church.

### 430. What are the matter and form of Matrimony?

The matter of Matrimony is the mutual consent of the spouses to give themselves to each other. The form consists in the words or actions through which the spouses express their consent to accept one another.

### 431. Who is the minister of the Sacrament of Matrimony?

The ministers of the Sacrament of Matrimony are the bride and groom themselves. Each confers the sacrament on the other, in the presence of a witnessing priest.

### 432. What is necessary for the worthy reception of Matrimony?

Matrimony should be received by persons in the state of grace, who understand the responsibilities of married life and follow the marriage laws of the Church.

433. **Regarding the celebration of Matrimony, what does the ordinary law of the Church require?**

The ordinary law of the Church requires that a Catholic be married in the presence of an authorized priest and before two witnesses. For serious reasons dispensations are granted from this law.

434. **Why does the Church make laws regarding the marriages of Catholics?**

The Church makes laws regarding the marriages of Catholics because she has authority from Christ over all the sacraments and other spiritual matters that affect baptized persons.

435. **Does the state have any authority regarding the marriages of baptized persons?**

Regarding the marriages of baptized persons, the state has the authority to make laws that pertain to the civil effects only.

436. **What is a Nuptial Mass?**

A Nuptial Mass is a Wedding Mass with special prayers to obtain God's blessings for the couple. Although such a Mass is not obligatory, it may be considered the most appropriate setting for the celebration of Matrimony.

### 437. Which are the effects of the Sacrament of Matrimony?

The effects of the Sacrament of Matrimony are: 1) an invisible bond that will last until the death of one of the spouses; and 2) the graces of the sacrament.

### 438. Which are the graces of the Sacrament of Matrimony?

When received in the state of grace, Matrimony increases sanctifying grace in the souls of the spouses and gives a special sacramental grace, which assures the couple of God's help to persevere together and grow in love, fidelity and holiness. This grace includes the right to: all the graces which are necessary to preserve mutual love in spite of anything and everything; the graces to bring children into the world and to raise them properly as good Christians; the graces to face and overcome all difficulties, misunderstandings, sicknesses or worries.

### 439. What would happen if one or both spouses were not in the state of grace at the time of their marriage?

A mortal sin of sacrilege would be committed. However, the couple would be truly married and with the subsequent restoration of friendship with God in the Sacrament of Penance, the graces of the sacrament would also be received.

## Preparation for Matrimony

**440. How should a Catholic prepare for marriage?**

A Catholic should prepare for marriage by praying for God's help in choosing a partner, by consulting his or her parents and confessor, by living a virtuous and chaste life, by receiving the Sacraments of Penance and Holy Eucharist often, and by attending Pre-Cana or similar courses offered in the diocese.

**441. Which qualities should one look for in a marriage partner?**

In a marriage partner one should look for: psychological compatibility; emotional stability; reverence for God and the teachings of the Church; kindness and understanding; uprightness; a spirit of industry and thrift.

**442. What are the "marriage banns"?**

The marriage banns are public announcements of an intended marriage. The purpose of the banns is to discover whether any impediments to the marriage exist. The new Code of Canon Law empowers the Conference of Bishops to establish rules for the publication of the banns.

### 443. What are meant by "impediments" to marriage?

Impediments are obstacles which can prevent a couple from marrying or can make a marriage unlawful.

### 444. Which impediments prevent a couple from validly marrying?

Some of these impediments are: lack of age, impotence, an existing valid marriage, sacred orders, close blood relationship, difference of religion in some cases and affinity.

### 445. Can the Church grant dispensations from these impediments?

The Church can grant dispensations from certain of these impediments but not from all.

### 446. If a couple marries without being aware of a serious impediment, is the marriage valid?

If a couple marries without being aware of a serious impediment, the marriage is invalid.

### 447. Can such a situation be remedied?

In many cases, such a situation can be remedied. A priest should be consulted and if necessary a dispensation obtained from the bishop. Then the marriage can be rectified, or "blessed." In other cases, the marriage is simply null—non-existent.

448. **When a marriage duly celebrated in the Church has been found to be null, are the children illegitimate?**
No, the children who were conceived or born before the marriage was found to be null are *legitimate* children of a *putative* marriage—that is, of a marriage that was thought to exist.

449. **What is a mixed marriage?**
A mixed marriage is a marriage between a Catholic and (strictly speaking) a baptized non-Catholic.

450. **Why does the Church urge Catholics to contract marriage only with Catholics?**
Married partners are called to perfect union of mind and communion of life, and this union can be broken or weakened when differences of opinion or disagreements touch on matters of religious truths and convictions.

451. **Is the same religion very important in the married state?**
Religion is such a vital force that when spouses cannot share it, they feel that

something important is missing from their union.

**452. May a dispensation be obtained so as to enter into a mixed marriage?**

Yes, a dispensation may be obtained from the bishop. Normally this is sought through the help of a priest-counselor.

**453. What must the Catholic party express in asking for this dispensation?**

The Catholic spouse must declare that he or she is ready to remove all dangers to his or her Faith. He or she also has the grave obligation to promise to have each of the children baptized and raised as a Catholic.

**454. What is the non-Catholic party's role in this regard?**

Before the marriage, the non-Catholic party has to be informed of the Catholic party's promise and obligations. He or she is to be well instructed regarding the purposes of Christian marriage, as well as its unity and indissolubility.

**455. Where and how should the ceremony of a mixed marriage be performed?**

The marriage is ordinarily to be performed before a duly authorized priest or deacon and two witnesses—otherwise it is invalid. (If a Catholic marries a non-Catholic of the Oriental Rite, the preceding provision is necessary for lawfulness, not for validity. But the presence of a sacred minister is required for validity.) However, a dispensation can be obtained from the bishop of the Catholic party. A Catholic priest (or deacon) and a non-Catholic minister may not officiate together at a mixed marriage, each performing his respective rite, nor can another religious ceremony be held either before or after the Catholic ceremony.

456. **If a serious difficulty prevents the ceremony of a mixed marriage from being performed in a Catholic church, what may be done?**
In the case of a serious difficulty, the bishop can permit the marriage to take place before a minister; without such a dispensation, the marriage would be invalid.

457. **May a Catholic validly marry a divorced person?**
A Catholic may not validly marry a divorced person, unless the latter's previous marriage was invalid.

## Unity and Indissolubility

### 458. Which are the chief characteristics of marriage?

The chief characteristics of marriage are unity and indissolubility. These characteristics apply to *all* marriages, for they are rooted in the law of God.

> "So they are no longer two but one. What therefore God has joined together, let no man put asunder" (Mt. 19:6).

### 459. What is meant by the unity of marriage?

By the unity of marriage is meant that neither husband nor wife may have a second or third marriage partner while the first partner is living. Marriage must be between one man and one woman.

### 460. What is adultery?

Adultery is the mortal sin of sexual intercourse between a married person and someone who is not his or her marriage partner.

### 461. What is meant by the indissolubility of marriage?

By the indissolubility of marriage is meant the lifelong, unbreakable nature of the marriage bond.

### 462. Is the indissolubility of marriage beneficial?

Yes. Its advantages include:
- —a sense of security;
- —mutual fidelity and mutual help;
- —domestic and social peace and order;
- —the procreation of children and their good upbringing.

### 463. What is civil divorce?

Civil divorce is the attempt to dissolve a marriage by the authority of civil law (cf. Mk. 10:2-12).

### 464. Can a valid and consummated marriage of baptized persons truly be dissolved by the authority of civil law?

A valid marriage can be truly dissolved only by the death of one of the spouses, or by the Church in certain exceptional circumstances—but never by a civil court.

### 465. Is separation ever permitted by the Church?

The Church permits a couple to separate for serious reasons, but without the right to remarry.

### 466. What are some reasons why the Church might grant permission to separate?

The reason for *perpetual* separation is adultery on the part of one of the partners. Other causes which permit the injured partner to seek a *temporary or indefinite* separation are: criminal or shameful conduct, the education of the children in schism or heresy, grave danger to soul and body. Normally, a priest should be consulted before the separation takes place.

### 467. Is civil divorce ever permitted?

Civil divorce with the right to remarry is never permitted by the Church because it is against the law of God. A civil divorce for legal reasons is sometimes permitted by the bishop, but neither partner may remarry while the first partner is living.

> To the married I give charge, not I but the Lord, that the wife should not separate from her husband (but if she does, let her remain single or else be reconciled to her husband)—and that the husband should not divorce his wife (1 Cor. 7:10-11).

### 468. What are some needs of today's separated and legally divorced Catholics?

Today's separated and legally divorced Catholic needs:

—special guidance not to become bitter against the laws of Christ;

—help to overcome feelings of loneliness and desolation;

—encouragement to receive the sacraments often, especially Holy Communion;

—encouragement never to enter into an invalid marriage, which cuts one off from the sacramental life of the Church.

"Whoever divorces his wife and marries another, commits adultery against her; and if she divorces her husband and marries another, she commits adultery" (Mk. 10:11-12).

### 469. What is recommended for a divorced Catholic who has remarried?

A divorced Catholic who has remarried must never lose hope or the sight of salvation. He or she should remain faithful to Sunday Mass and personal prayer. It is a difficult way to live and reach salvation—but the mercy of God is great, especially to the contrite heart. He or she should also ask for reliable counsel.

### 470. What is an annulment?

An annulment, or decree of nullity, is a decision by a marriage tribunal that an apparently valid marriage was actually invalid from the beginning, because of the existence of some impediment or other invalidating obstacles.

471. **Following a valid annulment, is a Catholic free to remarry?**
Yes, following a valid annulment a Catholic is free to remarry.

## Children

472. **Can one validly enter into marriage with the intention of not having children?**
One cannot validly enter into marriage with the intention of not having children, since the procreation (and education) of children is one of the two primary purposes of marriage, given by God.

473. **Are Catholic couples obliged to have as many children as possible?**
No, Catholic couples are obliged only to act in a truly responsible manner in bringing children into the world and raising them well. This responsibility includes the recognition of the procreation of children as one of the fundamental purposes of marriage and the avoidance of abortion and artificial birth control as contrary to God's law.

474. **Is marriage rendered invalid by childlessness?**
A valid marriage is not rendered invalid by unforeseen circumstances. Therefore,

if a couple married with the intention of accepting the children God would send them, childlessness does not render the marriage invalid.

## Duties of the Married

**475. Which are the chief duties of spouses to one another?**

The chief duties of the spouses to one another are: 1) fidelity; 2) cohabitation; and 3) mutual assistance. Fidelity means that each partner in a marriage is bound to refrain from any activity proper only to marriage with anyone other than the spouse. Cohabitation means that a husband and wife should live together and may separate temporarily and usually with mutual consent only for sufficiently important reasons. Mutual assistance means friendship and mutual love.

**476. Which are the special duties of the husband?**

The special duties of the husband are to exercise his God-given authority with love, kindness and respect toward his wife and toward his children.

> Husbands, love your wives, as Christ loved the church and gave himself up for her... (Eph. 5:25).

> Fathers, do not provoke your children, lest they become discouraged (Col. 3:21).

DSP

**May God keep husbands and
wives faithful in marriage
and grant them the joy of living
to see their children's children.**

**477. Which are the special duties of the wife?**
The special duties of the wife are to agree with her husband in everything that is not sinful and to be loving, devoted and generously dedicated to her children and to the care of her home.

> Wives, be subject to your husbands, as to the Lord. For the husband is the head of the wife as Christ is the head of the church, his body, and is himself its Savior. As the church is subject to Christ, so let wives also be subject in everything to their husbands... (Eph. 5:22-24).

**478. How can couples accomplish their duties and persevere in love until the end of their lives?**
To accomplish their duties and persevere in love until the end of their lives, couples are to ask God for the lifelong assistance of His grace, which is necessary in order to meet their responsibilities as husband and wife and as Christian parents.

## CHRISTIAN FAMILY LIFE

### Basic Facts About the Family

**479. What is the family?**
The family is the oldest natural society on earth and the irreplaceable basic unit of all human society.

### 480. How did the family originate?

The family was instituted by God Himself as an intimate community of life and love and was consecrated by Jesus Christ during His life on earth.

> "From the beginning of creation, 'God made them male and female.' 'For this reason a man shall leave his father and mother and be joined to his wife, and the two shall become one.' So they are no longer two but one. What therefore God has joined together, let not man put asunder" (Mk. 10:6-9).

### 481. What is the essential role of the family?

The essential role of the family is to communicate, nourish and guard life and love.

### 482. Which are the four general tasks of a family?

The four general tasks of a family are: to form a loving community of persons; to welcome and serve life; to cooperate in the betterment of society; and to share in the life and mission of the Church.

### 483. What role does marriage play in a family?

Marriage is the foundation of the family, since marriage and conjugal love are ordained to the procreation and education of children.

**484. Are husband and wife equal?**
Yes, husband and wife are perfectly equal as regards human dignity, even though God has made them physically and psychologically different.

> Then the Lord God said, "It is not good that the man should be alone; I will make him a helper fit for him" (Gn. 2:18).

> You husbands, live considerately with your wives, bestowing honor on the woman as the weaker sex, since you are joint heirs of the grace of life, in order that your prayers may not be hindered (1 Pt. 3:7).

**485. Who is head of the family?**
The husband is head of the family, as Christ is the head of the Church (cf. Eph. 5:22-23).

**486. What is the wife's role in the family?**
The wife is the heart of the family (cf. Sir. 36:24).

## The Family as a Community

**487. How did Jesus spend the greatest part of His life on earth?**
Jesus spent the greatest part of His life on earth living and working in a human family.

**488. What is the best model for families?**
The Holy Family—Jesus, Mary and Joseph —is the best model for every Christian

family. It gives the best example of the family virtues practiced to perfection through sacrifice and selfless giving.

### 489. What is the home meant to be?

The home is meant to be the privileged place of love and of training in the continual and progressive self-giving of husband and wife to each other.

> Let each one of you love his wife as himself, and let the wife see that she respects her husband (Eph. 5:33).

### 490. Whose responsibility is it to make the family a loving communion of persons?

All family members, each according to his or her own gift, have the grace and responsibility of making the family a loving communion of persons.

### 491. How can family unity be preserved and made perfect?

Family unity can only be preserved and made perfect by a spirit of selfless love on the part of the members.

> Do nothing from selfishness or conceit, but in humility count others better than yourselves. Let each of you look not only to his own interests, but also to the interests of others (Phil. 2:3-4).

### 492. Which fundamental attitudes should be found in the family?

The fundamental attitudes which should be found in the family are faithfulness, love and respect.

**493. How are family trials and difficulties to be met?**

Family trials and difficulties are to be met with full confidence and trust in God. He permits all things for our greater good and always gives the graces to cope with them.

**494. How should we view our own family?**

While respecting *all* families, we should love our own above all and do our best to make it always more pleasing to God.

## Duties of Parents and Children

**495. Which is the fundamental right of the offspring?**

The primary right of the offspring is the right to life: thus, every child that is conceived has the right to be born and to receive generous concern, even if the child is sickly or handicapped.

**496. What attitude should the Christian family have toward children?**

A Christian family should have the greatest esteem for each child's personal dignity, and an attitude of acceptance, love, respect and concern for his or her material, emotional and spiritual welfare.

> Lo, sons are a heritage from the Lord,
> the fruit of the womb a reward
> (Ps. 127:3).

### 497. How are children a blessing to a married couple?

Children are a living reflection of a couple's love, a permanent sign of their unity and a living synthesis of their fatherhood and motherhood.

### 498. Should parents' love for their children resemble God's love?

Yes, parents' love for their children is meant to be a visible sign of the love of God Himself for each of their children.

### 499. To whom does the task of bringing up and educating children belong?

The task of bringing up and educating children is to be the joint concern of the father and the mother.

### 500. Which are the natural duties of parents toward their children?

The duties of a mother to her child begin as soon as she realizes she is pregnant, because she must begin to abstain from anything that might injure the fetus. From the time of the baby's birth to the point at which he or she is able to provide for himself, the parents have the obligation of providing for their child's physical and intellectual needs. Important for the emotional growth of the children is the parents' avoidance of favoritism.

**501. Which are the religious duties of parents toward their children?**

Parents should have their children baptized soon after birth. They are to give them instruction regarding the truths of faith and morals, supervision and help in fulfilling religious and moral obligations, good advice and especially good example. Parents should send their children to Catholic schools whenever possible; when this cannot be done they must see to it that the children receive adequate religious instruction in a CCD program or through some other means.

**502. Why does the Church call for the religious training of children both in the home and in parish programs?**

The Church calls for the religious training of children in both home and classroom because of the non-religious and anti-religious influences of our culture, to which the children are widely exposed.

**503. Why does the Church place such great emphasis on the Confirmation of children and adolescents and on the study of Catholic teaching before and after receiving this sacrament?**

The Church places such great emphasis on Confirmation and the study of Catholic teaching before and after receiving this sacrament because in our secular society this is extremely important for living our Faith, sharing it and defending it when necessary.

> Guard the truth that has been entrusted to you by the Holy Spirit who dwells within us (2 Tm. 1:14).

> Prove yourselves innocent and straightforward, children of God beyond reproach in the midst of a twisted and depraved generation—among whom you shine like the stars in the sky (Phil. 2:15 NAB).

### 504. How can children contribute to building a Christian family?

Children can and are to contribute to building a Christian family by loving, respecting and obeying their parents.

> He who fears the Lord honors his father,
>     and serves his parents as rulers
>         (Sir. 3:7 NAB).

> Children, obey your parents in the Lord, for this is right. "Honor your father and mother" (this is the first commandment with a promise), "that it may be well with you and that you may live long on the earth" (Eph. 6:1-3).

### 505. How should corrections be given?

Corrections should be given with firm kindness, without anger or threats, so they will accomplish their goal of making the children better.

> He who spares the rod hates his son,
>> but he who loves him is diligent to discipline him (Prv. 13:24).

> Fathers, do not provoke your children to anger, but bring them up in the discipline and instruction of the Lord (Eph. 6:4).

### 506. How should corrections be taken?

Corrections should be taken with gratitude, never with anger and resentment, since they are given for our greater good.

> A wise son hears his father's instruction,
>> but a scoffer does not listen to rebuke (Prv. 13:1).

> If a son ceases to hear instruction,
>> he wanders from words of knowledge (Prv. 19:27 NAB).

### 507. What should parents teach teenagers about sex?

Parents should teach teenagers that sex is a precious gift given by God to enable husband and wife to share in His creative action. Because of this God-given purpose it is mortally sinful to use sex outside of marriage.

### 508. Should teenagers also be enlightened by parents about the occasions leading to sins of sex?

Parents have the duty to enlighten their children that whatever is done by oneself or with others to arouse the passions of sex outside marriage is grievously sinful.

"If your right eye causes you to sin, pluck it out and throw it away; it is better that you lose one of your members than that your whole body be thrown into hell" (Mt. 5:29).

Do not be deceived: "Bad company ruins good morals" (1 Cor. 15:33).

Immorality and all impurity or covetousness must not even be named among you, as is fitting among saints (Eph. 5:3).

## 509. How can parents help their teenagers to keep pure?

Parents can help their teenagers to keep pure by educating them to pray and to often receive the Sacraments of Penance (Reconciliation) and Holy Eucharist, in which Jesus can give them what nature cannot give: the strength not to fall, or the strength to rise again.

## 510. What should the problem of loss of faith in many youths teach parents?

This widespread problem should teach parents to explain to their teenagers, as early as possible, that Christian morality is meant by God to form upright men and women, whose reward is a serene life and a preparation for attaining total personal fulfillment in whatever state in life they will embrace.

## The Family and Holiness

### 511. What is another name for the Christian family?

The Christian family is often called and truly is the "domestic church," a unique and irreplaceable community of persons that is like the Church in miniature.

### 512. Are the married called to holiness?

All persons, including married persons, are called to become saints by fulfilling the duties of their state in life according to God's will and in cooperation with His grace. Many of the Church's canonized saints were married.

> For this is the will of God, your sanctification... (1 Thes. 4:3).

### 513. Should the holiness of the Christian family influence others?

Yes, the Christian family is meant to be a leaven in society, a sign of God's presence in the world.

### 514. How can the family radiate its holiness and act as a leaven in society?

Each member is called to live a truly Christian life where he lives, works, studies or plays. All, as individuals or as a family, should take part, according to the possibilities, in the lay apostolate of the Church and in fostering the missions.

## Family Spirituality

### 515. Is there a family spirituality?

Yes, there is a family spirituality outlined by St. Paul and quoted by Pope John Paul II in an address to families: "Put on, then...compassion, kindness, humility, meekness, and patience, forbearing one another and...forgiving each other.... And above all these put on love, which binds everything together in perfect harmony. And let the peace of Christ rule in your hearts, to which indeed you were called in the one body. And be thankful!" (Col. 3:12-15)

### 516. What is humility?

Humility is the moral virtue which enables us to acknowledge our total dependence on God as His creatures and to recognize whatever good there is in us as a gift from God for us to use to do good and for which we must give an account.

> What have you that you did not receive? If then you received it, why do you boast as if it were not a gift? (1 Cor. 4:7)

### 517. What is patience?

Patience is the moral virtue which enables one peacefully and serenely to endure difficulties and annoyances caused by others, for the love of God and to gain heaven.

A patient man need stand firm but for a
time,
    and then contentment comes back to him
    (Sir. 1:20 NAB).

**518. How should material goods be viewed?**
While we may work to better our family
financially, we should always avoid giving greater importance to the accumula-
tion of material goods rather than to the
family's spiritual progress.

"Do not seek what you are to eat and what
you are to drink, nor be of anxious mind.
For all the nations of the world seek these
things; and your Father knows that you
need them. Instead, seek his kingdom, and
these things shall be yours as well" (Lk.
12:29-31).

**519. On what is the love in a family based?**
The love in a family is based on faithfulness and generosity, on tenderness,
self-control, and patient understanding,
and is constantly renewed at the supernatural sources.

**520. Which are the supernatural sources that
renew love in a family?**
The supernatural sources that renew love
in a family are prayer and the sacraments, especially Reconciliation (Penance), Mass and Holy Communion.

### 521. Why is family prayer important?

Family prayer is important because it gives strength to overcome the unavoidable family problems and difficulties, is a source of unity, and obtains the grace needed to practice continual virtue.

### 522. Which prayer is ideally suited for a family to pray together?

The prayer ideally suited for a family to pray together is the rosary, which can easily be learned and prayed by members of all ages.

### 523. How should a family spend Sunday?

Sunday should be spent in worship, healthful relaxation and, in general, in ways that promote union with God and family unity and harmony.

## The Vocations of the Children

### 524. What should parents do to help their children prepare for their future?

Parents should provide their children with a good education, not only physical, but especially religious, moral and intellectual, and encourage them in following their aptitudes. They should especially foster among their children religious and priestly vocations, while leaving them, however, free to make their own ultimate choice.

**525. What is meant by a religious vocation?**
A religious vocation is a special calling from God to follow Jesus by living the three evangelical counsels.

**526. Which are the evangelical counsels?**
The evangelical counsels are voluntary poverty, chastity for the sake of the kingdom of God, and more perfect obedience. They were pointed out by Jesus as the way of perfection, and He first lived them.

**527. Who follow the evangelical counsels?**
The evangelical counsels are followed by religious priests, by brothers, by sisters, and by the members of secular institutes. The commitment to this sacred way of life is made through vows or promises. For religious, profession is public; for members of secular institutes, it is private.

**528. How are religious and priestly vocations fostered in the family?**
Vocations to the priestly or religious life are nourished through family prayer, the example of faith and the support of love.

**529. How many states in life are there?**
Among the faithful by divine institution there exist in the Church sacred ministers who are called clerics (bishops,

priests, deacons), and other Christian faithful who are called laity. From both groups there exist faithful who are consecrated to God through the profession of the evangelical counsels.

## The Wider Family

### 530. How should in-laws be treated?
In-laws should be treated with gratitude, respect and charity.

> "Honor your father-in-law and your mother-in-law; they are now your parents" (Tb. 10:12).

### 531. Why does a family owe gratitude and respect to the grandparents?
A family owes gratitude and respect to grandparents because from them the family received existence, education and support, all of which have often been bought with suffering and hard work.

> With all your heart honor your father,
>> and do not forget the birth pangs of your mother.
> Remember that through your parents you were born;
>> and what can you give back to them that equals their gift to you? (Sir. 7:27-28)

### 532. How are grandparents a blessing to a family?
Grandparents are a blessing to a family because they are a witness to the past, a

source of wisdom for the young, and often have the gift of bridging generation gaps before they might develop.

533. **What can grandparents do to enrich the family?**

Grandparents can enrich the family through prayer, wise counsel, and the help they are able to give.

534. **With what attitude should grandparents fulfill their role in the family?**

Grandparents should fulfill their role in the family with serenity and joy, giving the example of sincere Christian living.

535. **Do we have obligations toward deceased family members?**

We do have obligations toward deceased family members. We must keep their memory alive and offer suffrages for them, especially the holy Sacrifice of the Mass.

## The Media of Communication

536. **What influence do the media of communication have on the family?**

The media can exercise a good influence on the life and habits of the family and on the education of children, but at the same time they often present dangers to faith and morals by promoting wrong ideologies and distorted ways of looking at life, the family, religion and morality.

Whatever is true, whatever is honorable, whatever is just, whatever is pure, whatever is lovely, whatever is gracious, if there is any excellence, if there is anything worthy of praise, think about these things (Phil. 4:8).

## 537. Should parents supervise children's reading and TV viewing?

Parents must supervise their children's reading and TV viewing, since they are responsible for the religious, moral and social education of their children.

## 538. What kind of books should be in a Catholic family's library?

Only those books should be kept that support the fundamental human and religious values that form part of the true good of society; books in which these values are ignored or deliberately attacked should be eliminated.

## 539. What kind of magazines should be in a Catholic home?

A Catholic home should purchase or subscribe to only those magazines that promote truth and an upright approach to religion and morality.

## 540. What kinds of programs should be viewed?

Only those programs should be viewed that do not harm the family in its existence, its stability, its balance and its happiness: in other words, whatever does not tear down or wear down the family's religious and moral values.

## 541. How much television should be watched?

Television viewing can be judged excessive when it disrupts family unity or begins to stunt the spiritual, intellectual, or physical development of the children.

## 542. What can be done to remove immoral television programs from the air?

Parents can and should influence the selection and preparation of television programs by contacting the broadcasting companies and those in charge of production, and informing them of their views and opinions.

# SACRAMENTALS

## 543. What is a sacramental?

Sacramentals are sacred signs which bear a resemblance to the sacraments: they signify effects, particularly of a spiritual kind, which are obtained through the

The sacramentals are sacred signs
which dispose us to receive the
chief effects of the sacraments.

Church's intercession. By them men are disposed to receive the chief effects of the sacraments, and various occasions in life are rendered holy.

### 544. Where does the name "sacramental" come from?

The sacramentals are so named because many of them are used in the celebration of the sacraments and also because they, too, like the sacraments, are external signs through which blessings are received from God.

### 545. How does a sacramental obtain blessings from God?

A sacramental obtains blessings from God by the prayers that the Church offers for those using the sacramental, and because of the devotion that the object, action or word inspires.

### 546. Which blessings are obtained through sacramentals?

Some blessings obtained from sacramentals are: actual graces; the forgiveness of venial sins; the removal of the temporal punishment deserved by our sins; health and other material blessings; defense against the devil.

### 547. How do the sacramentals differ from the sacraments?

The sacramentals were instituted by the Church, while the sacraments were instituted directly by Christ; the sacramentals obtain grace through the prayers of the Church, while the sacraments operate by the direct action of Christ; the sacramentals are partly dependent on the faith and good dispositions of the person using them, while the sacraments operate by the direct power of Christ.

### 548. Why did the Church institute the sacramentals?

The Church instituted the sacramentals to add more dignity to the ritual of the sacraments, to help us to receive the sacraments with better dispositions, and to inspire us to live more devoutly.

### 549. Which are two of the principal sacramentals?

Two of the principal sacramentals are the liturgical year and the Liturgy of the Hours.

### 550. What is the liturgical year?

The liturgical year is a sacred time embracing the whole year: from the first Sunday of Advent to the last Sunday of Ordinary Time. It is a sacramental because it has been established by the Church to make us reflect on the mystery of our salvation and thus be inspired to live our life in conformity with the life of our Redeemer.

### 551. Into how many seasons is the liturgical year divided?

The liturgical year is divided into five seasons:

1) Advent: we prepare for the coming of Christ at Christmas and at the end of the world;

2) Christmas Season: we adore Christ in His birth, infancy and hidden life;

3) Lent: we commemorate our Lord's passion and death for our sins;

4) Easter Season: we celebrate the greatest event of the year, the resurrection of the Lord, His ascension into heaven, and Pentecost;

5) Ordinary Time: we reflect at length on the teachings of Christ during this period of thirty-three to thirty-four weeks, which begins after the Christmas Season and is resumed after Pentecost.

### 552. What is the Liturgy of the Hours?

The Liturgy of the Hours is the public prayer of the Church, made obligatory for the clergy and for religious men and women according to their rules and recommended to the laity. Its purpose is to sanctify the whole day through the praising of God at certain hours. The Liturgy of the Hours consists of morning prayer, daytime prayer, office of readings, evening prayer and night prayer.

### 553. Which are some actions that are sacramentals?

Some actions that are sacramentals are: genuflecting, kneeling, bowing the head, making the Sign of the Cross, folding the hands, sprinkling with holy water.

### 554. Which blessed objects are the sacramentals most used by Catholics?

The blessed objects most used by Catholics as sacramentals are holy water, crucifixes, rosaries, medals, statues, scapulars, candles, blessed ashes and blessed palms.

### 555. Why do we use holy water?

We use holy water to remind ourselves of our baptism, to ask for the forgiveness of our sins, and to implore God to protect us from all evils and dangers to soul and body.

# Christian Morality

## CONSCIENCE

### 556. What is conscience?

Conscience is the mind's practical judgment as to whether an action, word, thought, desire or omission is good and may be consented to, or evil and must be avoided. Conscience is the most secret core and sanctuary of a man, where he is alone with God.

> Beloved, if our hearts do not condemn us, we have confidence before God (1 Jn. 3:21).

### 557. Must we follow our conscience?

When, after diligent reflection, we are certain that something is the right thing to do, we must follow our conscience.

### 558. Are we truly responsible for our actions?

We are truly responsible for our actions because God gave us an intellect and free

Ryan Miller Photography

"Conscience is man's most secret core, and his sanctuary. There he is alone with God, whose voice echoes in his depths."
—Church in the Modern World

will and we are to use them to fulfill the purpose for which He made us.

> The soul that sins shall die. The son shall not suffer for the iniquity of the father, nor the father suffer for the iniquity of the son; the righteousness of the righteous shall be upon himself, and the wickedness of the wicked shall be upon himself (Ez. 18:20).

### 559. What is a right conscience?

A right conscience is one in conformity with the natural and divine law, and in full agreement with the Church's teachings, which authentically interpret God's law.

### 560. How can a right conscience be formed?

A right conscience can be formed by praying for the light of the Holy Spirit and by understanding the motives of the moral law in order to embrace it with a deeper knowledge and love of God.

### 561. What is a doubtful conscience?

A doubtful conscience is a conscience which cannot decide for or against the morality of an act. One must either refrain from acting or resolve the doubt.

### 562. What is a scrupulous conscience?

A scrupulous conscience is a conscience that is constantly in doubt, in dread of sin where there is none, or in dread of mortal sin where there is only venial sin.

### 563. How can a scrupulous conscience be cured?

A scrupulous conscience can be cured by obedience to a wise and good confessor. Sometimes medical help is also called for.

### 564. What is a lax conscience?

A lax conscience is a conscience that judges more by convenience than by God's law and easily commits sin, slight or serious, by judging everything carelessly, without thought of the consequences and the offense to God.

### 565. What if "everyone else is doing it"?

"Everyone else is doing it" is not a good excuse for our own wrongdoing, since God's law is not based on popularity, but on His divine will and man's final end.

> I appeal to you, brethren, to take note of those who create dissensions and difficulties in opposition to the doctrine which you have been taught; avoid them. For such persons do not serve our Lord Christ, but their own appetites, and by fair and flattering words they deceive the hearts of the simple-minded (Rom. 16:17-18).

### 566. Is everything that is legal, morally right?

Everything that is legal is not necessarily morally right. We are only obliged to obey laws that are in accord with God's law, and must never obey those which violate God's law, even if they are legal in a human court.

> We must obey God rather than men (Acts 5:29).

### 567. Does a good end ever justify the use of evil means?

No, we are never permitted to do evil in order that good may result from it. God wants us to have a good end and reach it by doing good deeds. Anyone, and especially a Christian, must be ready to make sacrifices and if necessary even choose death in order to save his or her soul.

### 568. If a conscience errs because of invincible ignorance, does the person sin?

No, if a conscience errs because of invincible (unavoidable) ignorance, the person does not sin.

### 569. Is it obligatory to form a right conscience?

Yes, it is a sacred obligation to form a right conscience, because our conscience is the means that God gave us to judge, here and now, what is good and therefore to be done, and what is evil and therefore to be avoided.

In the ten commandments God teaches us
what is for our good.

# THE TEN COMMANDMENTS

## 570. Which are the two great commandments?

The two great commandments are: You shall love the Lord your God with all your heart, and all your soul, and with all your mind, and with all your strength; you shall love your neighbor as yourself for the love of God.

> "You shall love the Lord your God with all your heart, and with all your soul, and with all your mind, and with all your strength. The second is this, 'You shall love your neighbor as yourself.' There is no other commandment greater than these" (Mk. 12:30-31).

## 571. How can we practice the two great commandments?

We can practice the two great commandments by fulfilling the decalogue, or ten commandments, which explains how to love God, self and neighbor.

> The commandments, "You shall not commit adultery, You shall not kill, You shall not steal, You shall not covet," and any other commandment, are summed up in this sentence, "You shall love your neighbor as yourself" (Rom. 13:9).

### 572. Where did the ten commandments come from?

God Himself gave the ten commandments to Moses (cf. Ex. 20:1-17). They set forth the natural law. The third commandment, which commands the worship of God and practice of religion, has the natural law for its basis; however, to give God external worship on a certain day belongs to the ceremonial law. God has ordained the ten commandments for the good of all mankind.

"Thus says the Lord, your redeemer,
   the Holy One of Israel:
'I, the Lord, your God,
   teach you what is for your good,
   and lead you on the way you should go'"
   (Is. 48:17 NAB).

### 573. Are the ten commandments relevant for Christians and the Gospel's law of love?

Yes, the ten commandments *are* relevant for Christians and the Gospel's law of love. Jesus proclaimed that He had come to *perfect* the commandments, not to abolish them: "Think not that I have come to abolish the law and the prophets; I have come not to abolish them but to fulfill them" (Mt. 5:17).

"Good Teacher, what must I do to inherit eternal life?" "...You know the commandments: 'Do not kill, Do not commit adultery, Do not steal, Do not bear false witness, Do not defraud, Honor your father and mother'" (Mk. 10:17, 19).

## 574. Which are the ten commandments?

The ten commandments are:

1. I, the Lord, am your God. You shall not have other gods besides me.
2. You shall not take the name of the Lord, your God, in vain.
3. Remember to keep holy the Lord's day.
4. Honor your father and your mother.
5. You shall not kill.
6. You shall not commit adultery.
7. You shall not steal.
8. You shall not bear false witness against your neighbor.
9. You shall not covet your neighbor's wife.
10. You shall not covet anything that belongs to your neighbor (cf. Ex. 20:1-17).

## 575. Can we always keep the ten commandments?

Yes. We can always keep the ten commandments, even when we are strongly tempted, because God will always help us if we ask Him in prayer.

> If you will, you can keep the commandments,
>> and to act faithfully is a matter of your own choice (Sir. 15:15).

R. Terra

**Give to the Lord glory and praise (Ps. 29).**

"Ask, and it will be given you; seek, and you will find; knock, and it will be opened to you. For every one who asks receives, and he who seeks finds, and to him who knocks it will be opened" (Mt. 7:7-8).

**576. Is it enough merely to keep the ten commandments?**

It is not enough merely to avoid breaking the ten commandments, for we should also be ready and willing to do whatever good we can for the glory of God and the good of neighbor in imitation of Jesus and the saints.

"And the King will answer them, 'Truly, I say to you, as you did it to one of the least of these my brethren, you did it to me'" (Mt. 25:40).

# THE FIRST COMMANDMENT

## "I, the Lord, am your God. You shall not have other gods besides me."

### Divine Worship

**577. Which is the first commandment?**

The first commandment is: I, the Lord, am your God. You shall not have other gods besides me (cf. Ex. 20:2-3).

### 578. What are we obliged to do by the first commandment?

By the first commandment we are obliged to love God above all things and to adore Him alone as our Creator and Lord.

> Hear, O Israel: The Lord our God is one Lord; and you shall love the Lord your God with all your heart, and with all your soul, and with all your might (Dt. 6:4-5).

### 579. What does it mean to love God above all things?

To love God above all things means to place Him and His law before everything else in our lives.

> "I delight to do your will, O my God;
> your law is within my heart" (Ps. 40:8).

### 580. How do we show God our love?

We show God our love by believing in Him and His teachings, trusting in His goodness, thanking Him, asking His forgiveness and help, doing penance for our sins and obeying His laws.

### 581. What does it mean to adore God?

To adore God means to worship Him with the reverence that is due to Him alone as our Creator and Lord.

> Ascribe to the Lord, O heavenly beings,
> ascribe to the Lord glory and strength.

Ascribe to the Lord the glory of his name;
worship the Lord in holy array
(Ps. 29:1-2).

## 582. Are we to pray to God privately or with others?

We are to pray to God both privately and with others, because we are social beings as well as individuals.

"When you pray, go into your room and shut the door and pray to your Father who is in secret..." (Mt. 6:6).

"Again I say to you, if two of you agree on earth about anything they ask, it will be done for them by my Father. For where two or three are gathered in my name, there am I in the midst of them" (Mt. 18:19-20).

## 583. Is any one form of worshiping God particularly important?

The Sacrifice of the Mass is particularly important for worshiping God.

...he holds his priesthood permanently, because he continues for ever. Consequently he is able for all time to save those who draw near to God through him, since he always lives to make intercession for them (Heb. 7:24-25).

## 584. What does God's first commandment forbid?

God's first commandment forbids atheism, idolatry, sacrilege, superstition, and participation in certain acts of non-Catholic worship.

## *Atheism and Idolatry*

### 585. What is atheism?

Atheism is the denial of God's existence and/or the following of a way of life which ignores God and His law.

> The fool says in his heart, "There is no God."
> They are corrupt, they do abominable deeds,
> there is none that does good (Ps. 14:1).

### 586. What does idolatry mean?

Idolatry means giving a creature the supreme honor that is due to God alone.

> "You shall not make for yourself a graven image, or any likeness of anything that is in heaven above, or that is in the earth beneath, or that is in the water under the earth; you shall not bow down to them or serve them; for I the Lord your God am a jealous God, visiting the iniquity of the fathers upon the children to the third and the fourth generation of those who hate me..." (Ex. 20:4-5).

### 587. How is something like idolatry commonly practiced today?

A sort of idolatry is commonly practiced today by giving the first place in our lives to self, another person, possessions, pleasures, money....

### 588. Is devil worship a form of idolatry?

Yes, devil worship is a form of idolatry—an extremely evil form—because it gives to God's enemy the worship that is due to God alone.

> Again, the devil took him to a very high mountain, and showed him all the kingdoms of the world and the glory of them; and he said to him, "All these I will give you, if you will fall down and worship me." Then Jesus said to him, "Begone, Satan! for it is written, 'You shall worship the Lord your God and him only shall you serve'" (Mt. 4:8-10).

## Sacrilege, Superstition, Non-Catholic Worship

### 589. What is sacrilege?

Sacrilege is the mistreatment of sacred persons, places or things, such as the sacraments.

> ...Judah has profaned the sanctuary of the Lord, which he loves... (Mal. 2:11).

### 590. What is superstition?

Superstition is attributing to a creature a power that belongs only to God—for example, making use of charms or spells, believing in dreams, fortune-telling or horoscopes, or going to spiritists.

> "Do not turn to mediums or wizards; do not seek them out" (Lv. 19:31).

### 591. Why is it wrong for Catholics to take part in certain acts of non-Catholic worship?

It is wrong for Catholics to take part in certain acts of non-Catholic worship whenever such activity implies belief in a religion that does not possess the fullness of God's truth and grace. Nonetheless, we should promote ecumenical activity whenever possible.

> I am amazed that you are so soon deserting him who called you in accord with his gracious design in Christ, and are going over to another gospel. But there is no other (Gal. 1:6-7 NAB).

## Honoring the Blessed Virgin and the Saints

### 592. Does God's first commandment allow us to honor and pray to the Blessed Virgin and the saints?

God's first commandment allows us to honor and pray to the Blessed Virgin and the saints; in fact, we are encouraged to do so.

> Their bodies were buried in peace,
>   and their name lives to all generations.
> Peoples will declare their wisdom,
>   and the congregation proclaims their
>   praise (Sir. 44:14-15).

> "For behold, henceforth all generations will call me blessed" (Lk. 1:48).

**593. What do we call the honor that we give to the Blessed Virgin and the saints?**

We call the honor that we give to the Blessed Virgin and the saints *veneration*, in contrast to the worship given only to God, which is *adoration*.

**594. Why do we honor the Blessed Virgin Mary in a special way?**

We honor the Blessed Virgin Mary in a special way because she is the Mother of God, and the Mother of the members of Christ's Body, the Church.

> "The Holy Spirit will come upon you, and the power of the Most High will overshadow you; therefore the child to be born will be called holy, the Son of God" (Lk. 1:35).

> When Jesus saw his mother, and the disciple whom he loved standing near, he said to his mother, "Woman, behold, your son!" Then he said to the disciple, "Behold, your mother!" And from that hour the disciple took her to his own home (Jn. 19:26-27).

**595. How does the Church honor the Mother of God?**

The Church honors the Mother of God with a special type of veneration in the liturgy and in various devotions. She encourages the faithful to know, imitate, love and pray to the Blessed Virgin in a special way.

**596. Does the Blessed Virgin pray for us?**
Yes, the Blessed Virgin prays for us, and her intercession is very powerful (cf. Jn. 2:1-11).

**597. Why does the Church honor the angels?**
The Church honors the angels: because by nature they hold a superior position among God's creatures; because they constantly adore the Holy Trinity; and because God has made them His special messengers to help us attain eternal salvation.

**598. Why do we honor and pray to the saints?**
We honor and pray to the saints because through God's grace they led holy lives, and in honoring them as God's friends we honor God Himself.

**599. How do we honor the saints?**
We honor the saints: by knowing about their lives; by imitating their virtues; by praying to them and asking them to pray to God for us; and by respecting their relics and images.

> Remember your leaders, those who spoke to you the word of God; consider the outcome of their life, and imitate their faith (Heb. 13:7).

> "...my servant Job shall pray for you, for I will accept his prayer not to deal with you according to your folly..." (Jb. 42:8).

**600. Why do we honor the bodies and relics of the saints?**

By honoring the bodies and relics of the saints, we are venerating not only their bodies or objects connected with them, but are venerating the person whose relic it is.

> And God did extraordinary miracles by the hands of Paul, so that handkerchiefs or aprons were carried away from his body to the sick, and diseases left them and the evil spirits came out of them (Acts 19:11-12).

## Images

**601. Does God's first commandment allow us to make or use statues and images?**

God's first commandment does allow us to make or use statues and images as long as they do not become objects of false worship.

**602. Why did God forbid the Hebrews to make graven images of Him?**

God forbade the Hebrews to make graven images because they lived among pagans and were very much inclined to imitate their idolatry.

**603. How should statues and images of Christ or the saints be treated?**

Statues and images of Christ or the saints should be treated with respect, just as we treat pictures of our loved ones with respect.

DSP

"To Your great Name be endless praise,
Immortal Godhead, One in Three."

**604. Do Catholics pray to crucifixes, relics, or holy images?**

When Catholics pray in front of crucifixes, relics or holy images, they are not praying to them, but to the persons they represent. Thus, Catholics adore Christ and venerate the saints.

## THE SECOND COMMANDMENT

### "You shall not take the name of the Lord, your God, in vain."

*Reverence in Speech*

**605. Which is the second commandment?**

The second commandment is: You shall not take the name of the Lord, your God, in vain (cf. Ex. 20:7).

**606. What are we obliged to do by the second commandment?**

By the second commandment we are obliged always to speak of God, the Blessed Virgin, the saints and sacred persons, places and things with reverence; to take oaths truthfully; and to be faithful in fulfilling promissory oaths and vows.

> Praise the Lord!
> Praise, O servants of the Lord,
> praise the name of the Lord!

Blessed be the name of the Lord from this
time forth and for evermore!
From the rising of the sun to its setting
the name of the Lord is to be praised!
(Ps. 113:1-3)

### 607. Why should we speak respectfully of sacred persons, places and things?

We should speak respectfully of sacred persons, places and things because they are consecrated to God.

### 608. What does the second commandment forbid?

The second commandment forbids profanity, blasphemy, cursing, and carelessness or deceit in the taking of oaths and the making of vows.

### 609. What is meant by profanity?

Profanity, or taking God's name in vain, means using the holy name of God, Jesus Christ, the Blessed Virgin, or the saints without reverence—as for example, to express anger or surprise.

"So you shall keep my commandments and do them: I am the Lord. And you shall not profane my holy name..." (Lv. 22:31-32).

### 610. Is it sinful to take God's name in vain?

It is sinful to take God's name in vain— usually venially sinful.

"...for the Lord will not hold him guiltless who takes his name in vain" (Ex. 20:7).

### 611. May the words of Sacred Scripture ever be used in a bad or worldly sense?

The words of Sacred Scripture may never be used in a bad or worldly sense. Neither should they be ridiculed, used in jokes or given any meaning other than what we believe God intended.

> ...we refuse to practice cunning or to tamper with God's word... (2 Cor. 4:2).

## Blasphemy and Cursing

### 612. What is blasphemy?

Blasphemy is any word, thought or action which shows deliberate contempt for God, the Blessed Virgin Mary, the angels, saints or religion. It is a serious sin if the blasphemer is truly aware of who God is.

> "Whoever curses his God shall bear his sin. He who blasphemes the name of the Lord shall be put to death" (Lv. 24:15-16).

### 613. What is cursing?

Cursing is invoking evil upon a person, place or thing.

> ...but no human being can tame the tongue—a restless evil, full of deadly poison. With it we bless the Lord and Father, and with it we curse men, who are made in the likeness of God. From the same mouth come blessing and cursing. My brethren, this ought not to be so (Jas. 3:8-10).

**614. Is it sinful to curse animals or things?**
It is sinful to curse animals or things, chiefly because of the uncontrolled anger or impatience involved.

**615. Is it sinful to curse another human being?**
Yes, it is sinful to curse another human being because he or she is made in the image and likeness of God.

> Bless those who persecute you; bless and do not curse them... (Rom. 12:14).

**616. Is it sinful to hope that some physical harm will befall a person in order to bring about his or her spiritual good, such as a return to the Faith?**
Such a hope is not sinful if it is motivated solely by charity.

## Oaths and Vows

**617. What is an oath?**
An oath is calling upon God to witness to the truthfulness of what we say.

> "You shall fear the Lord your God; you shall serve him, and swear by his name" (Dt. 6:13).

**618. When is an oath lawful?**
An oath is lawful: if we have a good reason for taking it; if we are sure we are speaking the truth; and if we do not have a sinful intention.

### 619. What constitutes a suitable reason for taking an oath?

The glory of God, the good of our neighbor or our own personal good would be a suitable reason for taking an oath.

> Men indeed swear by a greater than themselves, and in all their disputes an oath is final for confirmation (Heb. 6:16).

### 620. What is perjury?

Perjury is the serious sin of swearing an oath falsely—deliberately asking God to be a witness to a lie.

> "And you shall not swear by my name falsely, and so profane the name of your God: I am the Lord" (Lv. 19:12).

> By the sin of their mouths and the word of their lips
> let them be caught in their arrogance,
> for the lies they have told under oath
> (Ps. 59:13 NAB).

### 621. Are we obliged to keep an oath taken in order to promise something wrong or impossible?

No, we are not obliged to keep a promissory oath, if the object is or becomes sinful or impossible.

> "...or if someone, without being aware of it, rashly utters an oath to do good or evil, such as men are accustomed to utter rashly, and then recognizes that he is guilty of such

an oath; then whoever is guilty in any of these cases shall confess the sin he has incurred" (Lv. 5:4-5 NAB).

### 622. Does an oath taken to observe a civil constitution oblige us to observe all laws unconditionally?

An oath taken to observe a civil constitution obliges us only if laws are not opposed to divine or ecclesiastical rights.

### 623. What is a vow?

A vow is a free and deliberate promise made to God, by which a person binds himself under pain of sin to do something especially pleasing to God.

> When you vow a vow to God, do not delay paying it... (Eccl. 5:4).

### 624. Are vows always public?

Vows are not always public. There are also private vows.

### 625. Which are the most common vows today?

The most common vows today are the vows of poverty, chastity and obedience made by members of religious communities.

### 626. May any of the religious vows be made by persons living in the world?

Religious vows are also made by the members of secular institutes and may even be made by private individuals, who should usually consult their confessor.

### 627. What must one remember before making a vow?

Before making a vow one must remember that he will be obliged to fulfill it.

> "When you make a vow to the Lord your God, you shall not be slack to pay it; for the Lord your God will surely require it of you, and it would be sin in you. But if you refrain from vowing, it shall be no sin in you. You shall be careful to perform what has passed your lips, for you have voluntarily vowed to the Lord your God what you have promised with your mouth" (Dt. 23:21-23).

### 628. Is an unlawful vow binding?

An unlawful vow is not binding, because it is sinful; such a vow should not have been made and is not to be kept.

## THE THIRD COMMANDMENT

### "Remember to keep holy the Lord's day."

*Participation in the Mass*

### 629. Which is the third commandment?

The third commandment is: Remember to keep holy the Lord's day (cf. Ex. 20:8).

DSP

On the day of the Lord the faithful
gather in church to offer with
the priest a true and perfect
sacrifice to God the Father.

630. **What are we obliged to do by the third commandment?**

By the third commandment we are obliged to worship God on Sundays and on holy days of obligation by participating in the holy Sacrifice of the Mass and by abstaining from all unnecessary servile work.

> "Offer to God a sacrifice of thanksgiving, and pay your vows to the Most High; and call upon me in the day of trouble; I will deliver you, and you shall glorify me" (Ps. 50:14-15).

631. **Why are we obliged to participate in the Mass rather than to simply worship God in our hearts?**

We are obliged to participate in the Mass because: 1) the Mass is the perpetuation of the sacrifice of Jesus on the cross, offered to the Father for our salvation; 2) we are composites of body and soul and need to worship God exteriorly as well as interiorly; 3) we are social beings and need to worship God with others as well as by ourselves.

632. **Is it necessary to be physically present at Mass?**

Yes, it is necessary to be physically present at Mass—which means present in the church or other place where the Mass is celebrated.

### 633. What is the purpose of televised Masses?

Televised Masses enable the sick or infirm and those who must care for them to follow the Mass in the only way possible for them. A televised Mass does not fulfill the Sunday obligation, but it is a great means of comfort and devotion for the sick and the elderly.

### 634. Has our Mass obligation been fulfilled if we have participated in only a portion of the Mass?

We should not miss a notable part of the Mass. To do so, or to arrive late or leave early, could be a sin.

### 635. At what age does the obligation of taking part in Sunday Mass begin?

The obligation of taking part in Sunday Mass begins when one reaches the use of reason—generally around the seventh year of age.

### 636. Is it a grave obligation to participate at Mass on Sundays?

Yes, the duty to participate at Mass on Sundays is a grave obligation unless one is excused because of a really good reason.

**637. Does a Saturday evening Mass fulfill the Sunday obligation?**

Yes, participation in a Saturday evening Mass that has the bishop's approval fulfills the Sunday obligation.

**638. Which is the best way of participating in the Sacrifice of the Mass?**

The best way of participating in the Sacrifice of the Mass is by offering it to God in union with the priest, offering ourselves to the Father with Christ the Victim, and receiving Him in Holy Communion.

**639. How is the unity of God's people expressed at Mass?**

The unity of God's people is expressed by the actions of the faithful who pray, sing and act together in the Mass. Most of all, it is expressed by the reception of the Holy Eucharist, which is the center of unity.

**640. Why was Sunday set aside as the Lord's day in place of the Sabbath of the Old Testament?**

Sunday was set aside as the Lord's day in place of the Sabbath of the Old Testament because of an apostolic tradition which took its origin from the day of Christ's resurrection.

On the first day of the week, when we were
gathered to break bread, Paul talked with
them, intending to depart on the morrow;
and he prolonged his speech until midnight
(Acts 20:7).

**641. Are we also obliged to attend Mass
on other days besides Sundays?**
We are also obliged to attend Mass on
the days which the Church has established as holy days of obligation.

## A Day of Rest

**642. What does the third commandment for-
bid?**
The third commandment forbids unnecessary servile work on Sundays and holy
days of obligation.

**643. What does servile work mean?**
Servile work means any work that requires
primarily physical, rather than mental,
labor, and is done for material purposes.

"Remember the sabbath day, to keep it
holy. Six days you shall labor, and do all
your work; but the seventh day is a sabbath
to the Lord your God; in it you shall not do
any work, you, or your son, or your daugh-
ter, your manservant, or your maidservant,
or your cattle, or the sojourner who is
within your gates; for in six days the Lord
made heaven and earth, the sea, and all

that is in them, and rested the seventh day; therefore the Lord blessed the sabbath day and hallowed it'' (Ex. 20:8-11).

**644. Which are some servile works?**

Some servile works are: mechanical and industrial work, field labor, business transactions.

**645. Why is servile work forbidden on Sundays and holy days of obligation?**

Servile work is forbidden on Sundays and holy days of obligation so that we may renew ourselves in body and in spirit, trusting that the Lord will provide for our needs if we obey His law. If done for a considerable time, or with grave scandal to others, unnecessary servile work is a grave sin.

**646. Is servile work ever permitted on Sundays and holy days of obligation?**

Servile work is permitted on Sundays and holy days of obligation if it is required by the service of God, our own real need or that of our neighbor.

**647. Which activities are permitted on Sundays and holy days of obligation?**

The activities that are permitted on Sundays and holy days of obligation are those which—although they may be tiring —are not servile works. They include: reading, writing, typing, teaching, draw-

G. Greganti

**Jesus—the model Son**

ing, embroidering, playing musical instruments, traveling, hunting, fishing, engaging in sports and games, cooking, caring for domestic or farm animals, performing duties that are necessary for the common good, and doing any good deed immediately connected with the relief of the poor or the service of God. Perhaps the best way to sum up our obligation to keep Sundays and holy days properly would be to say, with the new Code of Canon Law (canon 1247), that we should abstain from any activity or business which hinders the worship to be given to God, the joy proper to the Lord's Day, or due relaxation of mind and body.

# THE FOURTH COMMANDMENT
## "Honor your father and your mother."

## *Children and Parents*

**648. Which is the fourth commandment?**

God's fourth commandment is: Honor your father and your mother (cf. Ex. 20:12).

**649. What are we obliged to do by the fourth commandment?**

By the fourth commandment we are obliged to love and respect our parents, to be obedient in all that is not against the commandments of God and the laws of the Church and to help them in any need.

> Listen to me your father, O children;
>> and act accordingly, that you may be kept in safety.
> For the Lord honored the father above the children,
>> and he confirmed the right of the mother over her sons.
> Whoever honors his father atones for sins,
>> and whoever glorifies his mother is like one who lays up treasure (Sir. 3:1-4).

Children, obey your parents in the Lord, for this is right. "Honor your father and mother" (this is the first commandment with a promise), "that it may be well with you and that you may live long on the earth" (Eph. 6:1-3).

## 650. What is the source and basis of parental authority?

The source of parental authority is God Himself and its basis is the debt we owe to our parents for bringing us into the world.

> With all your heart honor your father,
>> and do not forget the birth pangs of your mother.
> Remember that through your parents you were born;
>> and what can you give back to them that equals their gift to you? (Sir. 7:27-28)

**651. How do children show their love and respect for their parents?**

Children show their love and respect for their parents when they speak and act with gratitude, try to please them, readily accept corrections, seek advice in important decisions, patiently bear with their parents' faults and pray for their parents.

> Hear, my son, your father's instruction, and reject not your mother's teaching... (Prv. 1:8).

> A wise son hears his father's instruction, but a scoffer does not listen to rebuke (Prv. 13:1).

**652. Are children obliged to obey their parents regarding their choice of state in life?**

Children should ordinarily seek the advice of their parents in regard to their choice of state in life, but they are not obliged to follow this advice if their parents are unreasonably opposed.

> "We must obey God rather than men" (Acts 5:29).

**653. After children have come of age, do they still have obligations to their parents?**

After children have come of age they are still obliged to love and respect their parents, and they have a serious obligation to care for them in time of need or in their old age.

> O son, help your father in his old age,
>     and do not grieve him as long as he lives;
> even if he is lacking in understanding,
>     show forbearance;
>     in all your strength do not despise him.
> For kindness to a father will not be
>         forgotten,
>     and against your sins it will be credited to
>         you;
> in the day of your affliction it will be
>         remembered in your favor;
>     as frost in fair weather, your sins will
>         melt away.
> Whoever forsakes his father is like a
>     blasphemer,
>     and whoever angers his mother is cursed
>         by the Lord (Sir. 3:12-16).

## 654. Which are the duties of parents towards their children?

Parents must take care of the spiritual and physical needs of their children: have them baptized and instructed well in the Faith, correct their defects, train them by word and example in the practice of Christian virtues, counsel and guide them in forming a correct moral conscience, and provide for their education and material welfare.

> Discipline your son, and he will give you
>     rest;
>     he will give delight to your heart
>         (Prv. 29:17).

> Fathers, do not provoke your children to anger, but bring them up in the discipline and instruction of the Lord (Eph. 6:4).

### 655. What does the fourth commandment forbid?

The fourth commandment forbids disobedience toward our parents and every form of disrespect, unkindness, stubbornness, spitefulness, wishing them evil, and violence.

> He who mistreats his father, or drives away his mother,
>> is a worthless and disgraceful son (Prv. 19:26).

## All Lawful Authority

### 656. Does the fourth commandment also oblige us to obey all lawful authorities?

Yes, all lawful authorities must be respected and obeyed—in everything that is not sinful—because all authority comes from God, as the Bible tells us.

> Let every person be subject to the governing authorities. For there is no authority except from God, and those that exist have been instituted by God. Therefore he who resists the authorities resists what God has appointed, and those who resist will incur judgment (Rom. 13:1-2).

### 657. Whom does the term "lawful authority" include?

The term "lawful authority" includes teachers, employers, public officials and Church leaders.

## Workers and Employers

**658. What are the duties of workers toward their employer?**

Workers must respect their employer and faithfully serve him according to their agreement.

**659. How should employers treat their workers?**

Employers should treat their workers with respect and fairness, remembering that the limited authority they have over them comes from God.

## Citizens and Public Officials

**660. What must a citizen do for his nation?**

A citizen must love his nation, be concerned for its welfare, obey just laws, respect the lawful authority, and cooperate and pray for progress and peace.

> First of all, then, I urge that supplications, prayers, intercessions, and thanksgivings be made for all men, for kings and all who are in high positions, that we may lead a quiet and peaceable life, godly and respectful in every way (1 Tm. 2:1-2).

**661. Which are the principal civic duties?**

The principal civic duties are: to vote with honesty and upright motives; to pay just taxes; to defend one's nation, even at the cost of one's life; to work for and support laws which protect Christian morals.

> For rulers are not a terror to good conduct, but to bad. Would you have no fear of him who is in authority? Then do what is good, and you will receive his approval, for he is God's servant for your good. But if you do wrong, be afraid, for he does not bear the sword in vain; he is the servant of God to execute his wrath on the wrongdoer. Therefore one must be subject, not only to avoid God's wrath but also for the sake of conscience. For the same reason you also pay taxes, for the authorities are ministers of God, attending to this very thing. Pay all of them their dues, taxes to whom taxes are due, revenue to whom revenue is due, respect to whom respect is due, honor to whom honor is due (Rom. 13:3-7).

> "Render therefore to Caesar the things that are Caesar's, and to God the things that are God's" (Mt. 22:21).

**662. Are we obliged to obey civil laws when they are contrary to God's law?**

If the civil law obliges citizens to violate the law of God, they must refuse to obey, for "we must obey God rather than men" (Acts 5:29).

**663. Which are the duties of Catholics with regard to voting?**

Catholics must vote for candidates who are conscientious and morally upright and whose beliefs and programs give promise of benefiting everyone.

**664. Is it a sin to vote for an enemy of religion or of the common good?**

It is a sin to vote for an enemy of religion or of the common good because by so doing one would voluntarily participate in the evil that the candidate would do if elected.

**665. Is it a sin not to vote?**

It could be a sin not to vote if this were to result in the election of an incompetent or evil candidate.

**666. Is the obligation of fighting for one's country binding upon all?**

In a just war, the obligation of fighting for one's country allows of exceptions only for reasons of conscience—provided also that these citizens (conscientious objectors) agree to serve the nation in some other way.

**667. What are the most important duties of public officials?**

The most important duties of public officials are justice in the exercise of their authority, and the promotion of the common good.

> He who rules should exercise his authority with care... (Rom. 12:8 NAB).

**668. Are the obligations of public officials serious ones before God?**

Yes, the obligations of public officials are serious ones before God, for they govern in His name and by His authority and are to render a strict account to Him.

> Give ear, you that rule over multitudes,
>     and boast of many nations.
> For your dominion was given you from the Lord,
>     and your sovereignty from the Most High,
>     who will search out your works and inquire into your plans.
> Because as servants of his kingdom you did not rule rightly,
>     nor keep the law,
>     nor walk according to the purpose of God,
> he will come upon you terribly and swiftly,
>     because severe judgment falls on those in high places.
> For the lowliest man may be pardoned in mercy,
>     but mighty men will be mightily tested (Wis. 6:2-6).

# THE FIFTH COMMANDMENT
## "You shall not kill."

### *Sins Against Life*

**669. Which is the fifth commandment?**

The fifth commandment is: You shall not kill (cf. Ex. 20:13).

"Forgive us the wrong we have done as we forgive those who wrong us" (Mt. 6:12).

## 670. What does the fifth commandment forbid?

God's fifth commandment forbids murder, abortion, genocide, infanticide, child abuse, euthanasia, sterilization and suicide, and all that can lead to spiritual or physical harm, whether of oneself or of others, such as anger, fighting, revenge, drunkenness, drug abuse, torments inflicted on body or mind, hatred and bad example.

> "You have heard that it was said to the men of old, 'You shall not kill; and whoever kills shall be liable to judgment.' But I say to you that every one who is angry with his brother shall be liable to judgment; whoever insults his brother shall be liable to the council, and whoever says, 'You fool!' shall be liable to the hell of fire" (Mt. 5:21-22).

## 671. What is abortion?

Abortion is the deliberate killing of an unborn child at any time after conception. Under any form, it is a grave crime, because it is the killing of an innocent human being, who has the same right to life as any other human person.

## 672. Does rape or incest justify abortion?

No, abortion is never justified, no matter what the cause of the child's conception.

### 673. What is "indirect abortion"?

"Indirect abortion" is not really abortion. It occurs as the result of a procedure in which the direct intention is to treat the mother who is in danger of death from a serious pathological condition, and in which the death of the fetus is an incidental, unintended and secondary result, which would have been avoided had it been possible. Every effort must be made to baptize the fetus.

### 674. What is euthanasia?

Euthanasia or "mercy killing" is willful murder or suicide in which a person's life is taken with the excuse of avoiding pain, shortening suffering, or eliminating someone who is supposedly useless to society because of old age, defect or illness.

> "You shall rise up before the hoary head, and honor the face of an old man, and you shall fear your God: I am the Lord" (Lv. 19:32).

### 675. Is it ever lawful to take the life of another person?

It can be lawful to take the life of another person when there is no other means to defend one's own life and goods of great value or those of our neighbor from an unjust aggressor. It can also be lawful to take the life of another person in a just war.

### 676. Does lawful public authority have the right to put a criminal to death?

Lawful public authority has the right to inflict capital punishment on criminals who have been lawfully convicted of grave crimes. Many Catholic thinkers, however, hold that capital punishment is not justified in our time.

> "He who kills a man shall be put to death" (Lv. 24:17).

### 677. Why is direct suicide sinful?

Direct suicide is sinful because God alone has the right over life and death, and the one who commits suicide, instead, takes his own life, thus assuming God's right, unless it can be presumed that he was not fully responsible for his act, which is very often the case.

> For you have power over life and death... (Wis. 16:13).

### 678. Is sterilization ever permitted?

Direct sterilization, done with the purpose of preventing conception, is never permitted and is always a grave sin, because it removes for selfish reasons the power of procreation given by God. Indirect sterilization, done to remedy a serious pathological condition, is justified.

### 679. Is abuse of alcohol and drugs sinful?

Abuse of alcohol and drugs is sinful because it can cause serious mental and physical damage and put one in the occasion of harming oneself and others.

> Who has woe? Who has sorrow?
> Who has strife? Who has complaining?
> Who has wounds without cause? Who has redness of eyes?
> Those who tarry long over wine, those who go to try mixed wine (Prv. 23:29-30).

### 680. What is scandal?

Scandal is giving another person—through one's words, actions, or omissions—the occasion of committing sin.

> "Woe to the world for temptations to sin! For it is necessary that temptations come, but woe to the man by whom the temptation comes!" (Mt. 18:7)

## Preserving Life

### 681. What does the fifth commandment oblige us to do with regard to physical life and health?

The fifth commandment obliges us to take the ordinary means to preserve our own life and health and that of our neighbor as far as we are able.

### 682. Are we obliged to take extraordinary means to preserve our life?

To preserve our life, we are not obliged to take extraordinary means which involve extreme difficulty.

### 683. Is the use of extraordinary means ever obligatory?

Extraordinary means are to be taken when the person is very necessary to his family, the Church or society.

### 684. May a person ever risk his own life or health?

A person may risk his own life or health if there is a proportionately serious reason—for example, to save the life of another person.

> "Greater love has no man than this, that a man lay down his life for his friends" (Jn. 15:13).

### 685. Is transplantation of vital organs ever permitted?

The Church permits transplantation of vital organs as long as the donor is already really dead, or would be able to live a normal life without the organ, as in the case of donating a kidney.

"The body is not meant for immorality,
but for the Lord, and the Lord
for the body" (1 Cor. 6:13).

# THE SIXTH AND
# NINTH COMMANDMENTS

## "You shall not commit adultery.
## You shall not covet your neighbor's
## wife."

### The Commandments About Purity

**686. Why are the sixth and ninth commandments treated together?**

The sixth and ninth commandments are treated together because they both deal with the virtue of purity: the sixth with external purity, and the ninth with interior purity.

### The Sixth Commandment

**687. Which is the sixth commandment?**

The sixth commandment is: You shall not commit adultery (cf. Ex. 20:14).

**688. What are we obliged to do by the sixth commandment?**

By the sixth commandment we are obliged to be pure and modest in behavior both when alone or with others.

> But immorality and all impurity or covetousness must not even be named among you, as is fitting among saints. Let there be no filthiness, nor silly talk, nor levity, which are not fitting; but instead let there be thanksgiving. Be sure of this, that no immoral or impure man, or one who is

covetous (that is, an idolater), has any inheritance in the kingdom of Christ and of God (Eph. 5:3-5).

### 689. What does the sixth commandment forbid?

The sixth commandment forbids impurity and immodest behavior, that is, the unlawful pleasures of sex and everything that leads to impurity.

Can a man carry fire in his bosom and his clothes not be burned?

Or can one walk upon hot coals and his feet not be scorched?

So is he who goes in to his neighbor's wife; none who touches her will go unpunished (Prv. 6:27-29).

### 690. What are some of the sins committed against the sixth commandment?

Some sins committed against the sixth commandment are adultery, fornication, contraception, homosexuality, prostitution, premarital sex, masturbation, and looking at indecent pictures, magazines, movies or TV programs.

Do you not know that the unrighteous will not inherit the kingdom of God? Do not be deceived; neither the immoral, nor idolaters, nor adulterers, nor homosexuals, nor thieves, nor the greedy, nor drunkards, nor revilers, nor robbers will inherit the kingdom of God (1 Cor. 6:9-10).

## *Fornication and Adultery*

### 691. What is fornication?

Fornication is sexual intercourse between an unmarried man and an unmarried woman. It is a grave sin because it
goes against the purpose given by God
to the conjugal act: it is to be used only
by married people for the purpose of
procreating children, when that is possible.

> Shun immorality. Every other sin which
> a man commits is outside the body; but
> the immoral man sins against his own body
> (1 Cor. 6:18).

### 692. What is adultery?

Adultery is sexual intercourse between a
married person and someone other than
his or her own spouse. It is a grave sin
against chastity and against justice.

> He who commits adultery has no sense;
>   he who does it destroys himself
>     (Prv. 6:32).

## *Contraception*

### 693. Why is contraception seriously sinful?

Contraception, or artificial birth control, is
seriously sinful because by practicing it the
couple rejects chaste married love and de-
fies God by wanting to increase pleasure
while avoiding their God-given respon-

sibility: the procreation of children. Moreover, by encouraging the irresponsible use of sex, artificial birth control has led to lack of respect for sex, the source of life, and for life itself.

**694. What about the Pill?**

The Pill is evil religiously, ethically and medically. It has already condemned numerous women to premature death, has impeded the conception of millions of offspring, has destroyed life in the womb, and has enticed many into immorality, with the danger of condemnation by God and the loss of eternal life.

## Natural Family Planning

**695. Are there methods of birth control that do not offend God?**

Yes, there are natural methods of birth control which do not offend God if used for right reasons.

**696. What is Natural Family Planning?**

Natural Family Planning is a name given to certain methods which are in accord with the harmonies which the Creator has impressed upon human nature. It uses no chemicals and no gadgets. It is based on sound scientific knowledge. It is completely harmless, reliable and healthful.

**697. Is Natural Family Planning morally and religiously acceptable?**

Natural Family Planning, rightly used, is both religiously and morally acceptable, because it accords with what both reason and revelation say about human nature and human sexuality.

**698. Why do we say "rightly used"?**

We say "rightly used," because:
—it requires use of intelligence and self-control;
—it should be used only when married people have serious motives for spacing out births.

**699. What might create serious reasons for spacing out births?**

Some serious reasons for spacing out births can derive from the physical or psychological conditions of husband or wife, or from external conditions. Selfishness, however, is a *sinful* motive.

**700. Can Natural Family Planning be abused?**

Natural Family Planning can be abused by those who want to use sex irresponsibly, either by fornication or by adultery. Reason and religion forbid both because of their sinfulness.

## *Homosexuality, Premarital Sex, Masturbation*

### 701. What is homosexuality?

Homosexuality is a grave sin against nature itself, because it is sexual activity with a person of the same sex, carried out for forbidden sexual pleasure. It goes directly against God's purpose in regard to the reproductive organs: "...Male and female he created them. And God blessed them, and God said to them, 'Be fruitful and multiply, and fill the earth and subdue it...'" (Gn. 1:28). It should be noted that while homosexual activity is forbidden, the homosexual condition, in itself, is not sinful.

### 702. What is premarital sex?

Premarital sex is sexual intercourse before marriage, founded on the error that in it consists the total commitment of the spouses-to-be. These nonmarital relations are very sinful, because the marital act is justified and sacred only between husband and wife.

### 703. What is masturbation?

Masturbation is the act of procuring complete sexual satisfaction by stimulating one's own sexual organs. Masturbation is a grave sin, because it goes against the divinely-ordained creative purpose of such organs.

## The Ninth Commandment

**704. Which is the ninth commandment?**

The ninth commandment is: You shall not covet your neighbor's wife (cf. Ex. 20:17).

**705. What are we obliged to do by the ninth commandment?**

By the ninth commandment we are obliged to be pure in our thoughts and desires.

> "But I say to you that every one who looks at a woman lustfully has already committed adultery with her in his heart" (Mt. 5:28).

**706. What does the ninth commandment forbid?**

The ninth commandment forbids all deliberate impure thoughts, intentions, imaginings, desires and feelings deliberately aroused or indulged in.

> Do you not know that you are God's temple and that God's Spirit dwells in you? (1 Cor. 3:16)

**707. Are all impure temptations sinful?**

Impure temptations are not sinful in themselves, but become sinful if they are deliberately aroused, indulged in, or consented to. They must be rejected at once.

"Now, you see, the Lord commands us to respect what belongs to others...."

## The Preservation of Chastity

**708. Which are the main dangers to chastity?**
The main dangers to chastity are laziness; unbridled curiosity; bad company; excessive drinking and drug abuse; immodest dress; indecent books, magazines, movies or TV programs; suggestive music and obscene talk (cf. Sir. 9:7-9).

**709. How can chastity be preserved?**
We can preserve chastity by avoiding dangers whenever possible, praying for God's help, frequently receiving the sacraments of Reconciliation (Penance) and Holy Communion, and cultivating a tender devotion to the Blessed Virgin Mary.

> "Watch and pray that you may not enter into temptation; the spirit indeed is willing, but the flesh is weak" (Mt. 26:41).

# THE SEVENTH AND TENTH COMMANDMENTS
## "You shall not steal.
## You shall not covet your neighbor's goods."

## Respect for Property

**710. Which is the seventh commandment?**
The seventh commandment is: You shall not steal (cf. Ex. 20:15).

### 711. Does everyone have a right to private ownership?

Yes, God has given everyone a right to private ownership, so that each might possess the fruits of his labors in some form, live in accord with his human dignity and maintain a degree of independence.

> "Neither shall you covet your neighbor's wife; and you shall not desire your neighbor's house, his field, or his manservant, or his maidservant, his ox, or his ass, or anything that is your neighbor's" (Dt. 5:21).

### 712. What are we obliged to do by the seventh commandment?

By the seventh commandment we are obliged to respect the property of others, to keep our business agreements, and to pay our debts.

### 713. What does the seventh commandment forbid?

God's seventh commandment forbids stealing, robbery, keeping what belongs to others, cheating, unjustly damaging someone's property, contracting debts beyond our means, and accepting bribes.

> "Woe to him who heaps up what is not his
> own—
>     for how long?—
> and loads himself with pledges!"
>     (Hab. 2:6)

## Stealing, Damaging, Cheating

### 714. How serious a sin is stealing?

Stealing is a serious sin if the thing stolen is of considerable value. Stealing something of small value can be mortally sinful if the owner is poor and thus suffers great injury. A series of small thefts could eventually result in a mortal sin, when the total amount taken becomes sufficiently large.

### 715. Must a thief return stolen goods?

Stolen goods or their value must be returned to the rightful owner if it is possible, or to his heir. If neither the owner nor his heir can be found, the goods or their value are to be given to the poor or to charitable causes. But restitution need not be made publicly.

> And Zacchaeus stood and said to the Lord, "Behold, Lord, the half of my goods I give to the poor; and if I have defrauded any one of anything, I restore it fourfold." And Jesus said to him, "Today salvation has come to this house..." (Lk. 19:8-9).

### 716. If we know or find out that we have purchased stolen goods, may we keep them?

No. We must restore such goods to their rightful owner, unless we have no way of locating him. Nor can we ask him to pay us for them. The only person from whom we can ask compensation is the person who sold the goods to us.

**717. May we keep what we find?**

If a thing is of moderate value, and we have made a reasonable effort to locate the owner, we may keep it. If it has great value, we should report the matter to the police.

**718. Is it wrong to keep what we have borrowed?**

Yes, it is wrong to keep what we have borrowed beyond the length of time established or agreed upon by the owner.

**719. Must one repair damage he has unjustly done to someone else's property?**

Yes, one must repair damage unjustly done to someone else's property or pay the cost of the damage as far as is possible.

**720. Which are some forms of cheating?**

Some forms of cheating are: negligence in working; tax evasion; false advertising; fraudulent contracts; false insurance claims; false representation of oneself as a person in need or as a collector for a charitable undertaking; copying in an examination.

"You shall do no wrong in judgment, in measures of length or weight or quantity. You shall have just balances, just weights..." (Lv. 19:35-36).

## Specific Obligations

**721. Which are the duties of workers in regard to the seventh commandment?**
Workers must conscientiously—in quality and quantity—do the work for which they are being paid, and guard against damage to the property of their employer.

> Make it a point of honor to remain at peace and attend to your own affairs. Work with your hands as we directed you to do (1 Thes. 4:11 NAB).

**722. May workers strike?**
Workers may strike only if: 1) negotiations regarding just claims have been sincerely attempted and have failed; 2) no serious harm to the common good or to the welfare of the workers themselves is foreseen; 3) no deliberate violence or force is used.

**723. Which are the duties of employers with regard to the seventh commandment?**
Employers must see to it that their workers are paid just wages, without undue delays that would cause hardship. They

are to see to it that working conditions are in accord with human dignity and are reasonably safe.

> To take away a neighbor's living is to murder him;
>> to deprive an employee of his wages is to shed blood (Sir. 34:22).

> Come now, you rich, weep and howl for the miseries that are coming upon you.... Behold, the wages of the laborers who mowed your fields, which you kept back by fraud, cry out; and the cries of the harvesters have reached the ears of the Lord of hosts (Jas. 5:1, 4).

### 724. Which are the specific obligations of manufacturers and dealers?

Manufacturers and distributors are to be honest in their presentation of the quality, quantity and purpose of the product they wish to sell, so that the customers will receive the right product. They are not to create unjust monopolies and sell goods at exhorbitant prices.

> Hear this, you who trample upon the needy,
>> and bring the poor of the land to an end,
> saying, "When will the new moon be over,
>> that we may sell grain?
> And the sabbath,
>> that we may offer wheat for sale,
> that we may make the ephah small and the shekel great,
>> and deal deceitfully with false balances,

that we may buy the poor for silver and the
needy for a pair of sandals, and sell the
refuse of the wheat?"
The Lord has sworn by the pride of Jacob:
"Surely I will never forget any of their
deeds" (Am. 8:4-7).

The people curse him who holds back
grain,
but a blessing is on the head of him who
sells it (Prv. 11:26).

## 725. Which are the obligations of judges, other public officials and candidates for public office?

Judges, other public officials and candidates for public office are not to accept bribes or to advance themselves (or favor special interests) by any other dishonest means. Moreover, they have a serious obligation to discharge their positions of trust with justice and diligence.

For I know how many are your transgressions,
and how great are your sins—
you who afflict the righteous, who take a
bribe,
and turn aside the needy in the gate
(Am. 5:12).

He who is greedy for unjust gain makes
trouble for his household,
but he who hates bribes will live
(Prv. 15:27).

### 726. What is usury?

Usury is lending at exhorbitant rates of interest. It has always been condemned by God and the Church.

> "...you take interest and increase and make gain of your neighbors by extortion; and you have forgotten me, says the Lord God" (Ez. 22:12).

> "If you lend money to any of my people with you who is poor, you shall not be to him as a creditor, and you shall not exact interest from him" (Ex. 22:25).

### 727. Can one who has broken the seventh commandment be absolved in confession if he does not intend to make restitution?

One who has broken the seventh commandment in a grave matter cannot be absolved in confession unless he intends to make restitution.

## Irresponsible Use of Money and Goods

### 728. In the name of justice, may the wealthy leave the poor destitute?

No, even if a wealthy person has a just claim on the possessions of a poor person he may not exercise it if by so doing he would leave the latter destitute.

> "If ever you take your neighbor's garment in pledge, you shall restore it to him before the sun goes down; for that is his only

covering, it is his mantle for his body; in what else shall he sleep? And if he cries to me, I will hear, for I am compassionate" (Ex. 22:26-27).

### 729. Can the principle of private ownership justify selfishness on the part of the wealthy?

No, no one is justified in keeping for his exclusive use what he does not need, while others are in dire lack.

He who has a bountiful eye will be blessed, for he shares his bread with the poor (Prv. 22:9).

### 730. Is it wrong to live beyond one's means?

It is wrong to live beyond one's means, if this is an injustice to one's creditors or to one's dependents.

### 731. What is gambling?

Gambling is the staking of money or valuables on a future event or on a game of chance, the result of which is unknown to the participants.

### 732. Is it wrong to gamble?

Gambling is not against Catholic moral standards if done with moderation. However, it can become a sin, even a mortal sin, if it leads to dishonesty or great risks to the welfare of one's family.

## *Desiring Others' Goods*

### 733. Which is the tenth commandment?

The tenth commandment is: You shall not covet anything that belongs to your neighbor (cf. Ex. 20:17).

### 734. What does "covet" mean?

"Covet" means to desire something that belongs to another. Covetousness is one of the seven capital sins.

### 735. What does the tenth commandment forbid?

God's tenth commandment forbids the willful desire to unjustly take or keep anything that belongs to others. It also forbids envy at another's success.

> "You shall not covet your neighbor's house; you shall not covet your neighbor's wife, or his manservant, or his maidservant, or his ox, or his ass, or anything that is your neighbor's" (Ex. 20:17).

### 736. Is it ever permissible to desire what belongs to another?

If the owner is willing for us to acquire his possession by his gift or through some other honest means, it is permissible for us to desire it.

# THE EIGHTH COMMANDMENT
## "You shall not bear false witness against your neighbor."

## Reputation

**737. Which is the eighth commandment?**

The eighth commandment is: You shall not bear false witness against your neighbor (cf. Ex. 20:16).

**738. What are we obliged to do by the eighth commandment?**

By the eighth commandment we are obliged always to tell the truth, especially when it concerns someone's good name and reputation, and to interpret the actions of our neighbor in the best way possible.

"You shall not utter a false report. You shall not join hands with a wicked man, to be a malicious witness" (Ex. 23:1).

**739. What does the eighth commandment forbid?**

The eighth commandment forbids false witnessing, lying, rash judging, rash suspicions, flattery, talebearing, detraction, calumny, contumely, libel, and the telling of secrets we are obliged to keep.

But now put them all away: anger, wrath, malice, slander, and foul talk from your mouth. Do not lie to one another, seeing that you have put off the old nature with its practices (Col. 3:8-9).

"If you remove from your midst oppression, false accusation and malicious speech...the Lord will guide you always" (Is. 58:9, 11).

### 740. What is a lie?

A lie is anything which we know or suspect to be untrue, said or done usually for the purpose of deceiving others.

Putting away falsehood, let every one speak the truth with his neighbor, for we are members one of another (Eph. 4:25).

### 741. Can lying be excused if done for a good reason?

No reason, however good, will excuse the telling of a lie, because a lie is always evil in itself: it deliberately expresses the opposite of what we know to be true, thus abusing our mind, which was meant for the truth.

One who rejoices in wickedness will be condemned (Sir. 19:5).

"He that would love life and see good days, let him keep his tongue from evil and his lips from speaking guile" (1 Pt. 3:10).

### 742. What is a jocose lie?

A jocose lie is a story made up in order to amuse or instruct others. It becomes sinful if the person telling it does not make it clear in some way that it is not to be taken literally.

### 743. What is a mental reservation?

A mental reservation is an evasion that is made when one is not conscience-bound to tell the entire truth. It can be used only with those who have no right to know the truth.

**744. Which mental reservations are permissible?**

Those mental reservations are permissible which give a clue as to the person's real meaning. Mental reservations which give no such clue are really lies and can never be permitted.

**745. Are there lies in actions as well as in words?**

Yes, there are lies in actions; this is what is meant by hypocrisy.

> Be not a hypocrite in men's sight,
>   and keep watch over your lips.
> Do not exalt yourself lest you fall,
>   and thus bring dishonor upon yourself.
> The Lord will reveal your secrets and cast
>   you down in the midst of the congregation,
> because you did not come in the fear of the
>   Lord,
>   and your heart was full of deceit
>   (Sir. 1:29-30).

**746. What is rash judging?**

Rash judging is believing something harmful to someone's character without having a sufficient reason.

**747. Why is it wrong to rash judge?**

It is wrong to rash judge because our neighbor is a person like us and has the right to our respect.

Therefore you have no excuse, O man, whoever you are, when you judge another; for in passing judgment upon him you condemn yourself, because you, the judge, are doing the very same things. We know that the judgment of God rightly falls upon those who do such things. Do you suppose, O man, that when you judge those who do such things and yet do them yourself, you will escape the judgment of God? (Rom. 2:1-3)

"Judge not, that you be not judged" (Mt. 7:1).

## Uncharitable Telling of the Truth

### 748. What is talebearing?

Talebearing is telling someone the unkind things that others have said about him or her.

### 749. Why is talebearing wrong?

Talebearing is wrong because it provokes a person to anger, bitterness, hatred, revenge and other sins.

> Curse the whisperer and deceiver,
>    for he has destroyed many who were at
>    peace (Sir. 28:13).

### 750. What is detraction?

Detraction is making known someone's secret faults without having a good reason to do so.

### 751. Why is detraction wrong?

Detraction is wrong because our neighbor has the right to his good name.

A good name is to be chosen rather than
great riches,
and favor is better than silver or gold
(Prv. 22:1).

### 752. Is one ever allowed to tell the hidden faults of another?

One is allowed to tell the hidden faults of
another when it is necessary to make
them known to the person's parents or
to authorities, so that the faults may be
corrected and the wrongdoer prevented
from committing greater faults.

## Calumny, Contumely, Libel

### 753. What is calumny?

Calumny is slander, that is, injuring
someone's reputation by telling lies.

O Lord, who shall sojourn in your tent?
Who shall dwell on your holy hill?
He who walks blamelessly, and does what
is right,
and speaks truth from his heart
(Ps. 15:1-2).

He who slanders his neighbor secretly
I will destroy (Ps. 101:5).

### 754. What is contumely?

Contumely is showing contempt for
someone by unjustly dishonoring him.

### 755. How may contumely be committed?

Contumely may be committed by ignor-
ing the person, by refusing to show the
proper signs of respect, by detraction or
by ridicule.

### 756. What is libel?

Libel is any false or malicious written or printed statement or any sign, picture or effigy tending to injure a person's reputation in any way.

## Secrets

### 757. Must we keep secrets?

We must keep secrets if we have promised to do so, if our office requires it, or if the good of others demands it.

> A newsmonger reveals secrets,
>     but a trustworthy man keeps a confidence (Prv. 11:13 NAB).
>
> Let anything you hear die within you;
>     be assured it will not make you burst (Sir. 19:9 NAB).

### 758. Does the seal of confession oblige anyone other than the priest?

The seal of confession strictly obliges anyone who may accidentally overhear or come to know matters dealt with in the confession of another person.

### 759. Is it ever permitted to read the letters or private writings of others?

The letters or private writings of others may never be read without permission from the owner, unless the motive is

ENIT

"He who hears you hears me" (Lk. 10:16).

to prevent grave harm to oneself, to another person or to society.

## Reparation

**760. What must we do if we sin against the eighth commandment?**

If we sin against the eighth commandment, we must repair the harm done as far as we are able. This obligation is especially present for one who is guilty of calumny.

# THE PRECEPTS OF THE CHURCH

## Specific Duties of Catholics

**761. Does the Catholic Church have the authority to make laws and precepts?**

Yes, the Catholic Church has the authority to make laws and precepts, because Jesus, her Founder, gave her this right when He told the Apostles, "Truly, I say to you, whatever you bind on earth shall be bound in heaven, and whatever you loose on earth shall be loosed in heaven" (Mt. 18:18).

**762. Why does the Catholic Church make laws and precepts?**

The Catholic Church makes laws and precepts, which prescribe certain acts of religion and penance, in order to apply the commandments of God and the teachings of the Gospel to the lives of the faithful.

**763. Who has the authority to make laws?**
The Pope and the bishops, as successors of the Apostles, have the authority to make laws (cf. Mt. 16:19; 18:18).

**764. Are we obliged to keep the precepts of the Church?**
All Catholics are obliged to keep the precepts of the Church.

**765. Which are some of the chief duties of today's Catholics?**
Some of the chief duties of today's Catholics are the following. (Those traditionally called precepts of the Church are marked with an asterisk and are in italics.)

1. To keep holy the day of the Lord's resurrection: *to worship God by participating in Mass every Sunday and holy day of obligation\*:* to avoid those activities that would hinder renewal of soul and body, e.g., needless work and business activities, unnecessary shopping, etc.

2. To lead a sacramental life: to receive Holy Communion frequently and the Sacrament of Penance regularly:

—to receive the Sacrament of Penance at least once a year*; (annual confession is obligatory only if serious sin is involved).

—minimally, to receive Holy Communion at least once a year, at Easter time, that is, between the First Sunday of Lent and Trinity Sunday.*

3. To study Catholic teaching in preparation for the Sacrament of Confirmation, to be confirmed, and then to continue to study and advance the cause of Christ.

4. To observe the marriage laws of the Church*: to give religious training (by example and word) to one's children; to use parish schools and religious education programs.

5. To strengthen and support the Church*: one's own parish community and parish priests; the worldwide Church and the Holy Father.

6. To do penance, including abstaining from meat and fasting from food on the appointed days.*

7. To join in the missionary spirit and apostolate of the Church (cf. "Basic Teachings," U.S. Bishops).

## Sundays and Holy Days

**766. Is it a grave obligation to go to Mass on Sundays and on holy days of obligation?**

Yes, it is a grave obligation to go to Mass on Sundays and holy days of obligation.

**767. Is there any other day on which this obligation can be fulfilled?**

Where approved, the Sunday or holy day obligation may be fulfilled by participating in the anticipated Mass of the evening before.

**768. Why do we have holy days of obligation?**

We have holy days of obligation to recall to our minds some of the sacred mysteries of our Catholic Faith and important events in the lives of Jesus, Mary, and the saints.

## Reconciliation and Eucharist

**769. What does it mean to receive the Sacrament of Penance or Reconciliation at least once a year?**

To receive the Sacrament of Penance or Reconciliation at least once a year means that we must make a good confession during the year. Generally this is done before the Easter Communion.

He who conceals his transgressions will not
prosper,
but he who confesses and forsakes them
will obtain mercy (Prv. 28:13).

### 770. What does it mean to receive Holy Communion at Easter time?

To receive Holy Communion at Easter time means (in the United States) to receive the Eucharist between the first Sunday of Lent and Trinity Sunday inclusive. Trinity Sunday is the Sunday after Pentecost.

"I am the living bread which came down from heaven; if any one eats of this bread, he will live for ever; and the bread which I shall give for the life of the world is my flesh" (Jn. 6:51).

### 771. If one has not received Holy Communion during Easter time, what should he do?

If he had a good reason for missing Holy Communion during Easter time, he should receive at some other time within the year, as the new Code prescribes (canon 920).

### 772. If one receives Holy Communion during the Easter time in the state of mortal sin, does he fulfill the precept?

If one receives Holy Communion during the Easter time in a state of mortal sin, he does not fulfill the precept; moreover, he commits a grave sin of sacrilege.

773. **What does the Church mean with the words "at least"?**

With the words "at least" the Church expresses the desire that we receive the Sacraments of Penance and Holy Eucharist frequently, because they help us to resist temptations, remain and grow in God's grace and know and correct our faults.

## Marriage Laws

774. **What is the ordinary marriage law of the Church?**

The ordinary marriage law of the Church is that a Catholic can contract a valid marriage only before an authorized priest or deacon and two witnesses.

775. **Does the Church sometimes grant a dispensation for a mixed marriage or a marriage between certain relatives?**

The Church can grant a dispensation for a mixed marriage or a marriage between certain relatives if there is sufficient reason for doing so.

776. **Why are marriages between a Catholic and a non-Catholic discouraged?**

Marriages between a Catholic and a non-Catholic are discouraged by the Church because mixed marriages are often a source of family difficulties, loss of faith, and poor instruction of the children in the Catholic Faith.

## Support of the Church

### 777. What does it mean to strengthen and support the Church?

To strengthen and support the Church means to do our share in helping to meet the financial needs of the Holy See, our diocese and our parish.

> Do you not know that those who are employed in the temple service get their food from the temple, and those who serve at the altar share in the sacrificial offerings? In the same way, the Lord commanded that those who proclaim the gospel should get their living by the gospel (1 Cor. 9:13-14).

## Penances

### 778. Why are there days of fast and abstinence?

The Church asks us to fast and abstain on certain days so that we may do penance for our sins, practice self-control, and lift our minds to spiritual things.

> "Yet even now," says the Lord,
> "return to me with all your heart,

> with fasting, with weeping, and with mourning;
> and rend your hearts and not your garments."
> Return to the Lord, your God,
> for he is gracious and merciful,
> slow to anger, and abounding in steadfast love (Jl. 2:12-13).

### 779. Which days are set aside for fast or abstinence?

Ash Wednesday and Good Friday are obligatory days of both fast and abstinence; the Fridays of Lent are obligatory days of abstinence.

> "The days will come, when the bridegroom is taken away from them, and then they will fast in that day" (Mk. 2:20).

### 780. What is a day of fast?

A day of fast is a day in which only one full meal is allowed with two other meals that do not together equal a full meal.

### 781. Who are obliged to fast?

Catholics between the ages of 21 and 59 are obliged to fast.

### 782. What is a day of abstinence?

A day of abstinence is a day on which we may not eat meat or soups and gravies made from meat.

### 783. Who are obliged to abstain?

Catholics over fourteen years of age are obliged to abstain.

**784. Why are the Fridays of Lent obligatory days of abstinence?**

The Fridays of Lent are obligatory days of abstinence to remind us that Jesus died on the cross for our sins on Good Friday.

**785. Are fasting and abstinence the only penances we should perform?**

Fasting and abstinence are not the only penances we should perform. The Church has lessened the number of days of fast and abstinence but asks us to undertake penances of our own choosing—such as attending daily Mass, performing charitable works and works of mortification—especially on Fridays and during the season of Lent. The substantial observance of the Days of Penance (Fridays) binds seriously; e.g. to omit all works of penance on all the Days of Penance would be a grave omission.

# THE LIFE OF VIRTUE

## *The Virtues*

**786. What is a virtue?**

A virtue is a habit of doing good.

**787. How many kinds of virtues are there?**

There are two main kinds of virtues: supernatural virtues, infused into the

DSP

"Through [Christ] we have gained access by faith to the grace in which we now stand.... We know that affliction makes for endurance, and endurance for tested virtue, and tested virtue for hope. And this hope will not leave us disappointed, because the love of God has been poured out in our hearts through the Holy Spirit who has been given to us" (Rom. 5:2-5).

soul by God, and natural virtues, acquired by repeating naturally good acts.

### 788. Which of the virtues are the most important?

The most important of the virtues are the three supernatural virtues that are called "theological."

## *The Theological Virtues*

### 789. What does "theological virtues" mean?

"Theological virtues" means that these virtues have God for their object and motive.

### 790. Which are the theological virtues?

The theological virtues are faith, hope and charity, or love.

> So faith, hope, love abide, these three; but the greatest of these is love (1 Cor. 13:13).

### 791. What is faith?

Faith is the supernatural virtue by which we believe all that God has revealed and teaches us through the Catholic Church, because He cannot deceive or be deceived.

### 792. Can we be saved by faith alone?

We cannot be saved by faith alone, because God also requires good works and St. James tells us in the Bible that "faith without works is dead."

> What does it profit, my brethren, if a man says he has faith but has not works? Can his

> faith save him? ...For as the body apart
> from the spirit is dead, so faith apart from
> works is dead (Jas. 2:14, 26).

### 793. How do we live by faith?

We live by faith by studying our Faith,
reading the Bible, believing God's revelation, and openly professing our Faith
when necessary.

> Now faith is the assurance of things hoped
> for, the conviction of things not seen. And
> without faith it is impossible to please him.
> For whoever would draw near to God must
> believe that he exists and that he rewards
> those who seek him (Heb. 11:1, 6).

### 794. How can a Catholic sin against faith?

A Catholic sins against faith by joining a
non-Catholic church, by denying a truth
of faith, by being indifferent to the Catholic religion, and by taking, in some
cases, active part in non-Catholic worship.

> ...Fight the good fight and hold fast to faith
> and a good conscience. Some men, by
> rejecting the guidance of conscience, have
> made shipwreck of their faith (1 Tm. 1:19
> NAB).

### 795. How can we protect our faith against dangers?

We can protect our faith by making
frequent acts of faith, by praying for an
increase of faith, by studying the truths
of faith, by living according to God's

will, by choosing friends and associates wisely, and by reading or viewing only good things—never anything against the teachings of the Church.

> Be watchful, stand firm in your faith, be courageous, be strong. Let all that you do be done in love (1 Cor. 16:13).

## 796. What is hope?

Hope is the supernatural virtue by which we trust that God will give us eternal life and all we need to obtain it, because He is merciful and faithful to His promises.

## 797. How do we live by hope?

We live by hope by trusting that God will give us the graces necessary for salvation.

> We rejoice in our sufferings, knowing that suffering produces endurance, and endurance produces character, and character produces hope, and hope does not disappoint us, because God's love has been poured into our hearts through the Holy Spirit who has been given to us (Rom. 5:3-5).

## 798. How can we sin against hope?

We can sin against hope by presumption and despair.

> And let us not grow weary in well-doing, for in due season we shall reap, if we do not lose heart (Gal. 6:9).

## 799. What is presumption?

Presumption is the sin of thinking that God will save us without any effort on our part, or of thinking that we do not need God's help to reach heaven.

> Guard against being presumptuous;
> be not as those who lack sense
> (Sir. 13:8 NAB).

## 800. What is despair?

Despair is the sin of deliberately refusing to believe that God will always give the necessary help for salvation to all who ask for it.

> We are afflicted in every way, but not crushed; perplexed, but not driven to despair (2 Cor. 4:8).

## 801. What is charity?

Charity is the supernatural virtue by which we love God above all as our Creator and Redeemer, and our neighbor as ourself for the love of God.

## 802. How do we live by charity?

We live by charity by living the two great commandments: that is, loving God with all our heart, soul, mind and strength, because He is worthy of all our love, and by loving our neighbor as ourself for the love of God. In practice this involves obeying the commandments of God and of the Church and performing the works of mercy.

Love is patient and kind; love is not jealous or boastful; it is not arrogant or rude. Love does not insist on its own way; it is not irritable or resentful; it does not rejoice at wrong, but rejoices in the right. Love bears all things, believes all things, hopes all things, endures all things (1 Cor. 13:4-7).

Love does no wrong to a neighbor; therefore love is the fulfilling of the law (Rom. 13:10).

## 803. How can we sin against charity?

We can sin against charity in many ways: by hating God or our neighbor, by envy, sloth, giving scandal, etc.

"You shall not bear hatred for your brother in your heart. Though you may have to reprove your fellow man, do not incur sin because of him. Take no revenge and cherish no grudge against your fellow countrymen. You shall love your neighbor as yourself. I am the Lord" (Lv. 19:17-18 NAB).

## *The Moral Virtues*

## 804. What is meant by "moral virtues"?

A moral virtue is a virtue that disposes us to treat others and ourselves in a way that is morally right.

## 805. Which are the most important moral virtues?

The most important moral virtues are religion, which helps us worship God worthily, and the cardinal virtues: prudence, justice, fortitude and temperance.

If one loves justice,
>    the fruits of her works are virtues;
> for she teaches moderation and prudence,
>    justice and fortitude,
>    and nothing in life is more useful for men
>       than these (Wis. 8:7 NAB).

## 806. What does the term "cardinal virtues" mean?

The word "cardinal" comes from the Latin word for "hinge." We call some virtues cardinal virtues because they support the other moral virtues as a door is supported on hinges.

## 807. What is prudence?

Prudence is the virtue which enables us to make right decisions about what must be done or not be done to attain our final end and the means to be used.

> Man, for all his splendor, if he have not prudence,
>    resembles the beasts that perish
>    (Ps. 49:21 NAB).

> Learn where prudence is,
>    where strength, where understanding;
> that you may know also
>    where are length of days, and life,
>    where light of the eyes, and peace
>    (Bar. 3:14 NAB).

## 808. What is justice?

Justice is the virtue which enables us to give God and all others their due, thus safeguarding the rights of God and man.

He who pursues justice and kindness
  will find life and honor (Prv. 21:21).

"Then render to Caesar the things that are
Caesar's, and to God the things that are
God's" (Lk. 20:25).

## 809. What is fortitude?

Fortitude is the virtue which enables us
to do what is right in the service of God
and the good of our neighbor, no matter
how difficult or dangerous it is, even at
the cost of life itself.

May you be strengthened with all power,
according to his glorious might, for all
endurance and patience with joy... (Col.
1:11).

I can do all things in him who strengthens
me (Phil. 4:13).

## 810. What is temperance?

Temperance is the virtue which enables
us to control our passions and desires,
and use things which please our senses
with self-control and moderation.

In whatever you do, be moderate,
  and no sickness will befall you
    (Sir. 31:22 NAB).

The grace of God has appeared, offering
salvation to all men. It trains us to reject
godless ways and worldly desires, and live
temperately, justly, and devoutly in this
age as we await our blessed hope, the
appearing of the glory of the great God and
of our Savior Christ Jesus (Ti. 2:11-13 NAB).

## 811. What is meant by passions?

The passions are strong inclinations of our soul—effects of original sin—which incline us to sin. They can and must be kept under control with prayer and will-power.

> Fall not into the grip of desire,
>    lest, like fire, it consume your strength (Sir. 6:2 NAB).

> And those who belong to Christ Jesus have crucified the flesh with its passions and desires (Gal. 5:24).

## 812. Which are some other moral virtues?

Other moral virtues are:

*Filial piety* and *patriotism*, which help us love, honor and respect our parents and nation;

*Obedience*, which helps us obey our parents and superiors, who represent God;

*Truthfulness*, or veracity, which helps us always tell the truth;

*Liberality*, which helps us use rightly the goods of this world;

*Patience*, which helps us to take trials and difficulties from the hands of God;

*Humility*, which helps us know ourselves and see that whatever is good in us comes from God;

*Chastity,* or purity, which helps us be pure in mind, heart and body.

There are many other moral virtues besides these.

## The Beatitudes

**813. What is meant by the eight beatitudes?**
The beatitudes are qualities that Jesus asks His followers to live by on their journey towards heaven.

**814. Which are the eight beatitudes?**
The eight beatitudes are:

1. Blest are the poor in spirit: the reign of God is theirs.

2. Blest too are the sorrowing; they shall be consoled.

3. [Blest are the lowly; they shall inherit the land.]

4. Blest are they who hunger and thirst for holiness; they shall have their fill.

5. Blest are they who show mercy; mercy shall be theirs.

6. Blest are the single-hearted for they shall see God.

7. Blest too the peacemakers; they shall be called sons of God.

8. Blest are those persecuted for holiness' sake; the reign of God is theirs (Mt. 5:3-10 NAB).

815. **Why does Jesus apply the term "blest" to the poor in spirit, the lowly, the sorrowing, etc.?**

Jesus calls such persons blest because they will be rewarded with peace of heart and conscience in this life, and everlasting happiness in the next.

## The Works of Mercy

816. **Are there any particular acts of virtue that Jesus recommended to everyone?**

Jesus recommended to everyone the corporal works of mercy (cf. Mt. 25:35-36) and, certainly, the spiritual works, which of their nature are even more perfect because they are directed to the soul of our neighbor, for his eternal salvation.

817. **Which are the most important corporal works of mercy?**

The most important corporal works of mercy are:

1. to feed the hungry;
2. to give drink to the thirsty;
3. to clothe the naked;
4. to visit the imprisoned;
5. to shelter the homeless;
6. to visit the sick;
7. to bury the dead.

818. **Which are the most important spiritual works of mercy?**
The most important spiritual works of mercy are:
1. to admonish the sinner;
2. to instruct the ignorant;
3. to counsel the doubtful;
4. to comfort the sorrowful;
5. to bear wrongs patiently;
6. to forgive all injuries;
7. to pray for the living and the dead.

819. **Can ordinary daily actions be true works of mercy?**
All the ordinary daily actions that relieve the corporal or spiritual needs of our neighbor are true works of mercy when we do them for the love of God.

820. **Are we all to perform works of mercy?**
We all are to perform works of mercy according to our own possibilities and the needs of our neighbor.

## Vices

821. **What is the opposite of virtue?**
The opposite of virtue is vice, which is the habit of doing evil, acquired by repeating bad actions.

**822. Which are the principal vices?**
The principal vices are the "seven capital sins." They are called capital sins because they are the source of other vices and sins.

**823. How can we overcome these vices?**
We can overcome these vices by striving to acquire the opposite virtues. The following is a guide:

       pride—humility;
       covetousness—justice and liberality;
       lust—chastity;
       gluttony—temperance;
       anger—meekness;
       envy—love of neighbor;
       sloth—love of God and diligence in
            His service.

# The Life of Prayer

## PRAYER

### 824. What is prayer?

Prayer is raising our minds and hearts to God, in loving conversation with Him.

> Hear, O Lord, when I cry aloud,
>   be gracious to me and answer me!
> You have said, "Seek my face."
>   My heart says to you,
> "Your face, Lord, do I seek."
>   Hide not your face from me (Ps. 27:7-9).

### 825. Why should we pray?

We should pray to offer God our Creator our loving adoration, to thank Him for His many blessings, to ask His forgiveness of our sins and to lessen our deserved punishment, and to beg for the graces we need.

> Have no anxiety about anything, but in everything by prayer and supplication with

Hoffman

"He would leave the city to spend the night on the Mount of Olives" (Lk. 21:37).

thanksgiving let your requests be made known to God. And the peace of God, which passes all understanding, will keep your hearts and your minds in Christ Jesus (Phil. 4:6-7).

### 826. How should we pray?

We should pray with an awareness of God's presence, with humility, confidence and perseverance.

> "Then you will call upon me and come and pray to me, and I will hear you. You will seek me and find me; when you seek me with all your heart, I will be found by you, says the Lord" (Jer. 29:12-14).

### 827. For whom should we pray?

We should pray for ourselves, for our loved ones, for enemies and sinners, for the holy souls in purgatory, for public officials, for bishops, priests, religious, the laity, and, in a special way, for the Pope.

### 828. Does God always hear our prayers?

God always hears our prayers if we pray well, because Jesus promised: "All you ask the Father in my name, he will give you" (Jn. 15:16 NAB).

### 829. Will God always give us what we pray for?

God will not always give us what we pray for, either because we did not pray well, or because He, as a loving Father, knows that what we asked for would not be good for us.

> We know that in everything God works for good with those who love him, who are called according to his purpose (Rom. 8:28).

### 830. What is mental prayer?
Mental prayer is prayer made interiorly with our mind, while uniting our heart to God.

### 831. What is vocal prayer?
Vocal prayer is praying with words, but we are to accompany our words with mind and heart.

### 832. What is an aspiration?
An aspiration is a short prayer.

### 833. Which prayers should every Catholic memorize?
Every Catholic should memorize at least the Our Father, the Hail Mary, the Glory Be to the Father, the Apostles' Creed, acts of faith, hope, love and contrition, and the rosary.

### 834. How should we begin and end our prayers?
We should begin and end our prayers with the Sign of the Cross.

**835. Why is the Sign of the Cross important?**

The Sign of the Cross is important because it expresses our belief in the unity and trinity of God, the Incarnation and our redemption by our Savior.

**836. How does the Sign of the Cross express these mysteries?**

"In the name" expresses our belief that there is only one God; "of the Father and of the Son and of the Holy Spirit" expresses our belief in the Trinity; tracing a cross on ourselves expresses our belief in our Redemption by the death of Jesus Christ on the cross.

**837. Are distractions in prayer sins?**

When they are deliberate, distractions in prayer could be venial sins. But if we refuse to dwell on them, they can even make our prayer more pleasing to God and more meritorious.

> Continue steadfastly in prayer, being watchful in it with thanksgiving (Col. 4:2).

**838. Is it good to use our own words in prayer?**

It is good and praiseworthy to use our own words in prayer, in intimate personal dialogue with God.

> Let us then with confidence draw near to the throne of grace, that we may receive mercy and find grace to help in time of need (Heb. 4:16).

PDDM

"One of his disciples asked him, 'Lord, teach us to pray....' He said to them, 'When you pray, say: "Father, hallowed be your name"'" (Lk. 11:1-2).

**839. What is the first thing we should do each morning?**

The first thing we should do each morning is thank God for a new day, make the Sign of the Cross, and say our morning prayers (cf. Ps. 5:2-4).

**840. What should be our last act of the day?**

Our last act of the day should be to say our night prayers, including an examination of conscience and an act of thanksgiving for the day (cf. Ps. 55:17-18).

# THE OUR FATHER

**841. Why is the Our Father a perfect prayer?**

The Our Father is a perfect prayer because Jesus Himself taught it to us, and because in it we ask first for God's glory and then for everything we need, spiritually and materially, both for ourselves and for all mankind, because God is the Father of all (cf. Mt. 6:9-13).

**842. When we say *"Our* Father" what do we mean?**

When we say *"Our* Father" we show that we are all children of the same heavenly Father; thus, we are reminded to pray not only for ourselves, but for all our brothers and sisters near and far.

### 843. What does "Our Father who art in heaven" mean?

"Our Father who art in heaven" means that God truly is our loving Father, our Creator, who cares for us and made us His adopted children through sanctifying grace and who, after this brief life, wants us in heaven with Him forever.

"If you then, who are evil, know how to give good gifts to your children, how much more will your Father who is in heaven give good things to those who ask him" (Mt. 7:11).

### 844. What does "hallowed be Thy name" mean?

"Hallowed be Thy name" means that we pray that everyone may know, respect and love God's holy name.

Praise the Lord!
  Praise, O servants of the Lord,
    praise the name of the Lord!
  Blessed be the name of the Lord from this
    time forth and for evermore!
  From the rising of the sun to its setting
    the name of the Lord is to be praised!
    (Ps. 113:1-3)

### 845. What does "Thy kingdom come" mean?

"Thy kingdom come" means that we pray that God's kingdom, which is a kingdom of love, justice and peace, may be spread all over the world, and that everyone may become members of the true Church and finally attain the kingdom of heaven.

846. **What does "Thy will be done on earth as it is in heaven" mean?**

"Thy will be done on earth as it is in heaven" means that we pray for ourselves and for everyone to do God's will as lovingly and promptly as the angels and saints do it in heaven.

847. **What does "Give us this day our daily bread" mean?**

"Give us this day our daily bread" means that we ask God to give us each day all the graces we need for our spiritual and material well-being.

> "Therefore do not be anxious, saying 'What shall we eat?' or 'What shall we drink?' or 'What shall we wear?' For the Gentiles seek all these things; and your heavenly Father knows that you need them all. But seek first his kingdom and his righteousness, and all these things shall be yours as well" (Mt. 6:31-33).

848. **What does "forgive us our trespasses as we forgive those who trespass against us" mean?**

"Forgive us our trespasses as we forgive those who trespass against us" means that we ask God to treat us just as we treat others, and to forgive us in the same way we forgive others.

Fra Angelico

"Hail Mary, full of grace,
the Lord is with thee."

"For if you forgive men their trespasses, your heavenly Father also will forgive you; but if you do not forgive men their trespasses, neither will your Father forgive your trespasses" (Mt. 6:14-15).

### 849. What does "lead us not into temptation" mean?

"Lead us not into temptation" means that we ask God to help us not to fall into temptation to sin, whether the temptation comes to us from the world, from our own passions, or from the devil.

### 850. What does "deliver us from evil" mean?

"Deliver us from evil" means that we ask God to protect us from all dangers to body and soul, especially from anything that would endanger our salvation.

### 851. What does "Amen" mean?

"Amen" means "it is true" or "so be it" and expresses our firm belief in all that the Our Father contains.

## THE HAIL MARY AND THE ROSARY

### 852. Where did the Hail Mary come from?

The first part of the Hail Mary consists of the greetings to Mary by the angel and Elizabeth, as recorded in the Bible; the second part was added by the Church under the guidance of the Holy Spirit.

> And he came to her and said, "Hail, full of grace, the Lord is with you!" (Lk. 1:28)
>
> And she exclaimed with a loud cry, "Blessed are you among women, and blessed is the fruit of your womb!" (Lk. 1:42)

### 853. Should we often pray the Hail Mary?

We should often pray the Hail Mary because it recalls the Incarnation of the Son of God for our salvation, honors Mary as the Mother of God, and asks for her help during our life and at the moment of our death.

### 854. What is the rosary?

The rosary is a "Gospel prayer" made up of Our Fathers, Hail Marys and Glorys, in which we meditate on important events in the lives of Jesus and Mary.

### 855. Does the Church recommend the recitation of the rosary?

The Church and all the recent Popes have highly recommended the recitation of the rosary as a means of advancing in the spiritual life and of obtaining peace for the world.

### 856. What other benefit can be gained from the rosary?

The rosary could also obtain the grace of a good death, because we ask Mary fifty times to "pray for us sinners now and at the hour of our death."

## THE SPIRITUAL LIFE AND THE BIBLE

**857. Which are the main enemies of our spiritual life?**
The main enemies of our spiritual life are the devil, the world and the flesh.

**858. How is the devil an enemy of our spiritual life?**
The devil is a powerful enemy who tries to make us sin so that we will lose our salvation.

> Be sober, be watchful. Your adversary the devil prowls around like a roaring lion, seeking someone to devour (1 Pt. 5:8).

**859. How is the world an enemy of our spiritual life?**
The world—that is, its pleasures—is an enticing enemy that draws us toward love of wealth, pleasure and power, rather than love of God and the spiritual life.

> For the sake of profit many sin,
>     and the struggle for wealth blinds the eyes (Sir. 27:1 NAB).

**860. How is the flesh an enemy of our spiritual life?**
The flesh is an enemy because of our weakened nature and our evil inclina-

"Whoever wishes to be my follower must deny his very self, take up his cross each day, and follow in my steps" (Lk. 9:23).

tions, which make it very difficult to control our passions.

> Let not the lustful cravings of the flesh master me,
> surrender me not to shameless desires (Sir. 23:6 NAB).

## 861. How can we overcome these enemies of our spiritual life?

These main enemies of our spiritual life can be overcome by reliance on God's grace, by prayer and by constant and careful vigilance.

> "Watch and pray that you may not enter into temptation; the spirit indeed is willing, but the flesh is weak" (Mk. 14:38).

## 862. What does it mean to take up our cross daily?

To take up our cross daily means to accept from the hands of God all the sufferings and trials He wills or permits in our daily lives to imitate our Savior who died on the cross for love of us.

> My son, if you come forward to serve the Lord,
> prepare yourself for temptation.
> Set your heart right and be steadfast,
> and do not be hasty in time of calamity.
> Cleave to him and do not depart,
> that you may be honored at the end of your life.
> Accept whatever is brought upon you,
> and in changes that humble you be patient.

> For gold is tested in the fire,
>> and acceptable men in the furnace of humiliation (Sir. 2:1-5).

### 863. What is meditation?

Meditation is a form of mental prayer in which we reflect on some truth of faith, a virtue or an event from the life of Christ or the saints, and try to make applications to our own daily life.

> Mary kept all these things, pondering them in her heart (Lk. 2:19).

### 864. Is daily meditation helpful in the spiritual life?

Daily meditation builds up spiritual life because it makes us grow in faith, hope and love and in the practice of all the virtues.

### 865. Is the reading of spiritual books helpful in the spiritual life?

The reading of spiritual books, especially the Bible, the lives of saints and other spiritual works, is essential to enlighten our mind, and to strengthen us in keeping our good resolutions.

### 866. What is the Bible?

The Bible is the book which contains the inspired Word of God. In it God speaks to us through the writings of men who were chosen by Him and guided by the Holy Spirit, so that they wrote only what He wanted them to write.

All scripture is inspired by God and profitable for teaching, for reproof, for correction, and for training in righteousness (2 Tm. 3:16).

**867. What are other names for the Bible?**
The Bible is also called "Sacred Scripture," which means "holy writings," or just "the Scriptures," or "the Word of God," since it is God's revelation to us.

**868. What is inspiration?**
Inspiration is the special guidance that the Holy Spirit gave to the Bible's human writers, so that they wrote everything God wanted them to write and only that, without any error.

**869. How is the Bible divided?**
The Bible is divided into the Old Testament with forty-six books, and the New Testament with twenty-seven books.

**870. What is the Old Testament?**
The Old Testament is the first part of the Bible, written before the birth of Jesus, which tells about the history and the preparation of the Hebrew people for the coming of the Savior, Jesus Christ.

**871. What is the New Testament?**
The New Testament is the second part of the Bible, written after the resurrection of Jesus, which tells about the birth, life,

teachings, passion, death, resurrection and ascension into heaven of Jesus Christ, and the life of the early Church.

### 872. What is the Gospel?

The Gospel, or "Good News," consists of the first four books of the New Testament, and gives us a detailed description of the life and teachings of Jesus. Because of this, these four books are the most important books of the Bible.

### 873. Can the Bible be mistaken?

The Bible cannot be mistaken since God Himself is the principal Author and He guided the human writers to write exactly what He wanted them to, and in the way He wanted them to. They wrote the truth that God wanted written down for the sake of our salvation.

### 874. Can we be mistaken in how we understand the Bible?

We can be mistaken in how we understand the Bible, and one of the reasons Jesus gave us the Church is so that it can explain and interpret the Bible with divine assistance the way He meant it.

> There are some things in them [St. Paul's letters] hard to understand, which the ignorant and unstable twist to their own destruction, as they do the other scriptures (2 Pt. 3:16).

875. **Can the Church make a mistake in interpreting the Bible?**

The Church can never make a mistake in authentically interpreting the Bible because the Holy Spirit preserves the Church from the possibility of making an error (cf. 2 Tm. 1:13-14).

876. **What does the Church take into consideration in interpreting the Bible?**

In interpreting the Bible, the Church considers the tradition of the Church Fathers and Doctors, the original languages, literary forms, the actual text, and historical findings, in order to reach the true meaning which the sacred author, under divine inspiration, had in writing and to avoid a purely fundamentalistic view which can be a false interpretation.

877. **How should we read the Bible?**

We should read the Bible humbly and prayerfully, and with a readiness to put God's Word into practice.

878. **Which are the books of the Bible?**

### OLD TESTAMENT

| Book | Abbrev. | Chap. |
|------|---------|-------|
| *The Pentateuch* | | |
| Genesis | Gn. | 50 |
| Exodus | Ex. | 40 |

| Book | Abbrev. | Chap. |
|------|---------|-------|
| Leviticus | Lv. | 27 |
| Numbers | Nm. | 36 |
| Deuteronomy | Dt. | 34 |

*The Historical Books*

| | | |
|------|---------|-------|
| Joshua | Jos. | 24 |
| Judges | Jgs. | 21 |
| Ruth | Ru. | 4 |
| 1 Samuel | 1 Sm. | 31 |
| 2 Samuel | 2 Sm. | 24 |
| 1 Kings | 1 Kgs. | 22 |
| 2 Kings | 2 Kgs. | 25 |
| 1 Chronicles | 1 Chr. | 29 |
| 2 Chronicles | 2 Chr. | 36 |
| Ezra | Ezr. | 10 |
| Nehemiah | Neh. | 13 |
| Tobit | Tb. | 14 |
| Judith | Jdt. | 16 |
| Esther | Est. | 10 |
| 1 Maccabees | 1 Mc. | 16 |
| 2 Maccabees | 2 Mc. | 15 |

*The Wisdom Books*

| | | |
|------|---------|-------|
| Job | Jb. | 42 |
| Psalms | Ps. | 150 |
| Proverbs | Prv. | 31 |
| Ecclesiastes | Eccl. | 12 |
| Song of Songs | Sg. | 8 |
| Wisdom | Wis. | 19 |
| Sirach | Sir. | 51 |

| Book | Abbrev. | Chap. |
|------|---------|-------|
| *The Prophetic Books* | | |
| Isaiah | Is. | 66 |
| Jeremiah | Jer. | 52 |
| Lamentations | Lam. | 5 |
| Baruch | Bar. | 6 |
| Ezekiel | Ez. | 48 |
| Daniel | Dn. | 14 |
| Hosea | Hos. | 14 |
| Joel | Jl. | 4 |
| Amos | Am. | 9 |
| Obadiah | Ob. | 1 |
| Jonah | Jon. | 4 |
| Micah | Mi. | 7 |
| Nahum | Na. | 3 |
| Habakkuk | Hb. | 2 |
| Zephaniah | Zep. | 3 |
| Haggai | Hg. | 2 |
| Zechariah | Zec. | 14 |
| Malachi | Mal. | 3 |

## NEW TESTAMENT

| Book | Abbrev. | Chap. |
|------|---------|-------|
| *The Historical Books* | | |
| Matthew | Mt. | 28 |
| Mark | Mk. | 16 |
| Luke | Lk. | 24 |
| John | Jn. | 21 |
| Acts of the Apostles | Acts | 28 |

| Book | Abbrev. | Chap. |
|------|---------|-------|
| *The Didactic Books* | | |
| Romans | Rom. | 16 |
| 1 Corinthians | 1 Cor. | 16 |
| 2 Corinthians | 2 Cor. | 13 |
| Galatians | Gal. | 6 |
| Ephesians | Eph. | 6 |
| Philippians | Phil. | 4 |
| Colossians | Col. | 4 |
| 1 Thessalonians | 1 Thes. | 5 |
| 2 Thessalonians | 2 Thes. | 3 |
| 1 Timothy | 1 Tm. | 6 |
| 2 Timothy | 2 Tm. | 4 |
| Titus | Ti. | 3 |
| Philemon | Phlm. | 1 |
| Hebrews | Heb. | 13 |
| James | Jas. | 5 |
| 1 Peter | 1 Pt. | 5 |
| 2 Peter | 2 Pt. | 3 |
| 1 John | 1 Jn. | 5 |
| 2 John | 2 Jn. | 1 |
| 3 John | 3 Jn. | 1 |
| Jude | Jude | 1 |
| *The Prophetic Book* | | |
| Revelation | Rv. | 22 |

# Prayers and Other Formulas

## The Sign of the Cross

In the name of the Father, and of the Son, and of the Holy Spirit. Amen.

## The Lord's Prayer

Our Father, who art in heaven, hallowed be Thy name; Thy kingdom come; Thy will be done on earth as it is in heaven. Give us this day our daily bread; and forgive us our trespasses as we forgive those who trespass against us; and lead us not into temptation, but deliver us from evil. Amen.

## Hail Mary

Hail Mary, full of grace! The Lord is with you; blessed are you among women, and blessed is the fruit of your womb, Jesus. Holy Mary, Mother of God, pray for us sinners, now and at the hour of our death. Amen.

## Glory to the Father

Glory to the Father, and to the Son, and to the Holy Spirit: as it was in the beginning, is now, and will be forever. Amen.

## The Angelus

The Angel of the Lord declared unto Mary.
And she conceived of the Holy Spirit.
*Hail Mary, etc.*
Behold the handmaid of the Lord.
May it be done unto me according to your word.
*Hail Mary, etc.*
And the Word was made flesh.
And dwelt among us.
*Hail Mary, etc.*
℣. Pray for us, O Holy Mother of God.
℞. That we may be made worthy of the promises of Christ.

Let us pray — O Lord, it was through the message of an angel that we learned of the incarnation of Your Son Christ. Pour Your grace into our hearts, and by His passion and cross bring us to the glory of His resurrection. Through the same Christ, our Lord. Amen.

*Glory to the Father, etc.*

## The Apostles' Creed

I believe in God, the Father Almighty, Creator of heaven and earth; and in Jesus Christ, His only Son, our Lord; who was conceived by the Holy Spirit, born of the Virgin Mary, suffered under Pontius Pilate, was crucified, died and was buried. He descended into hell; the third day He arose again from the dead; He ascended into heaven, sits at the right hand of God, the Father Almighty; from thence He shall come to judge the living and the dead. I believe in the Holy Spirit, the Holy Catholic Church, the communion of saints, the forgiveness of sins, the resurrection of the body, and life everlasting. Amen.

## An Act of Faith

O my God, I firmly believe that You are one God in three Divine Persons, Father, Son, and Holy Spirit; I believe that Your Divine Son became man and died for our sins, and that He will come to judge the living and the dead. I believe these and all the truths which the Holy Catholic Church teaches, because You have revealed them, who can neither deceive nor be deceived.

## An Act of Hope

O my God, relying on Your infinite goodness and promises, I hope to obtain pardon of my sins, the help of Your grace, and life everlasting, through the merits of Jesus Christ, my Lord and Redeemer.

## An Act of Love

O my God, I love You above all things, with my whole heart and soul, because You are all good and worthy of all love. I love my neighbor as myself for the love of You. I forgive all who have injured me, and I ask pardon of all whom I have injured.

### An Act of Contrition

O my God, I am heartily sorry for having offended You, and I detest all my sins, because of Your just punishments, but most of all because they offend You, my God, who are all good and deserving of all my love. I firmly resolve, with the help of Your grace, to sin no more and to avoid the near occasions of sin.

### Morning Offering

O Jesus, through the Immaculate Heart of Mary, I offer You all my prayers, works, joys and sufferings of this day, for all the intentions of Your Sacred Heart, in union with the Holy Sacrifice of the Mass throughout the world, in reparation for my sins, for the intentions of all our associates, and for the general intention recommended this month.

### Prayer Before Meals

Bless us, O Lord, and these Your gifts, which we are about to receive from Your bounty, through Christ our Lord. Amen.

### Prayer After Meals

We give You thanks for all Your benefits, O almighty God, who lives and reigns forever;

and may the souls of the faithful departed, through the mercy of God, rest in peace. Amen.

## Prayer Before a Crucifix

Behold, my beloved and good Jesus, I cast myself upon my knees in Your sight, and with the most fervent desire of my soul I pray and beseech You to impress upon my heart lively sentiments of faith, hope and charity, with true repentance for my sins and a most firm desire of amendment; while with deep affection and grief of soul I consider within myself and mentally contemplate Your five most precious wounds, having before my eyes that which David, the prophet, long ago spoke about You, my Jesus:

"They have pierced my hands and my feet; I can count all my bones" (Ps. 22:17-18).

## Hail, Holy Queen

Hail, holy Queen, Mother of Mercy, our life, our sweetness, and our hope! To you we cry, poor banished children of Eve; to you we send up our sighs, mourning and weeping in this valley of tears. Turn then, O most gracious advocate, your eyes of mercy toward us, and after this, our exile, show unto us the blessed fruit of your womb, Jesus. O clement, O loving, O sweet Virgin Mary.

## *Memorare*

Remember, O most gracious Virgin Mary, that never was it known that anyone who fled to your protection, implored your assistance or sought your intercession, was left unaided. Inspired with this confidence, we fly to you, O Virgin of virgins, our Mother; to you we come; before you we kneel, sinful and sorrowful. O Mother of the Word Incarnate, despise not our petitions, but in your clemency hear and answer them. Amen.

## *The Mysteries of the Rosary*

> *These mysteries—which present themselves as scenes, pictures and stories, one after another—lead you to an intellectual vision of the facts of the life of Jesus and Mary recorded in the mysteries, and to an understanding of the most sublime truths of our religion: the Incarnation of the Lord, the redemption, and the Christian life, present and future.* —Pope Paul VI

### Joyful Mysteries

(MON. AND THURS.)

1. Annunciation of the Angel to Mary (*Humility*)
2. Mary's Visit to Her Cousin Elizabeth (*Love of Neighbor*)
3. Birth of Jesus in the Stable of Bethlehem (*Spirit of Poverty*)

4. Presentation of Jesus in the Temple
   *(Obedience to God's Will)*
5. Jesus Is Found Again among the Doctors
   in the Temple *(Fidelity to Vocation)*

**Sorrowful Mysteries**     (TUES. AND FRI.)

1. Jesus Prays at Gethsemane *(Spirit of Prayer)*
2. Jesus Is Scourged at the Pillar *(Modesty)*
3. Jesus Is Crowned with Thorns
   *(Purity of Mind and Heart)*
4. Jesus Carries the Cross to Calvary
   *(Patience in Suffering)*
5. Jesus Dies for Our Sins
   *(Love for the Mass)*

**Glorious Mysteries**
                    (WED., SAT. AND SUN.)

1. Jesus Rises from the Dead *(Faith)*
2. Jesus Ascends into Heaven
   *(Desire for Heaven)*
3. The Holy Spirit Descends on the Apostles
   *(Wisdom, Fortitude, Zeal)*
4. The Mother of Jesus Is Assumed into
   Heaven *(Holy Life, Holy Death)*
5. Mary Is Crowned Queen of Heaven and
   Earth *(Final Perseverance)*

## *Angel of God*

Angel of God, my guardian dear, to whom God's love entrusts me here, ever this day be at my side to light and guard, to rule and guide. Amen.

## Eternal Rest

Eternal rest grant to them, O Lord, and let perpetual light shine upon them. May they rest in peace. Amen.

## The Sacraments

Baptism                  Anointing of the Sick
Confirmation             Holy Orders
Holy Eucharist           Matrimony
Penance

## The Great Commandments

1. You shall love the Lord your God
   with your whole heart,
   with your whole soul,
   and with all your mind.
2. You shall love your neighbor as
      yourself (Mt. 22:37-39).

## The Ten Commandments

1. I, the Lord, am your God. You shall not have other gods besides me.
2. You shall not take the name of the Lord, your God, in vain.
3. Remember to keep holy the Lord's day.
4. Honor your father and your mother.
5. You shall not kill.
6. You shall not commit adultery.

7. You shall not steal.
8. You shall not bear false witness against your neighbor.
9. You shall not covet your neighbor's wife.
10. You shall not covet anything that belongs to your neighbor.

## *Other Duties of Catholic Christians*

1. To keep holy the day of the Lord's resurrection: to worship God by participating in Mass every Sunday and holy day of obligation: to avoid those activities that would hinder renewal of soul and body, e.g., needless work and business activities, unnecessary shopping, etc.

2. To lead a sacramental life: to receive Holy Communion frequently and the Sacrament of Penance regularly:

—minimally, to receive the Sacrament of Penance at least once a year (annual confession is obligatory only if serious sin is involved);

—minimally, to receive Holy Communion at least once a year, at Easter time, that is, between the First Sunday of Lent and Trinity Sunday.

3. To study Catholic teaching in preparation for the Sacrament of Confirmation, to be confirmed, and then to continue to study and advance the cause of Christ.

4. To observe the marriage laws of the Church: to give religious training (by example

and word) to one's children; to use parish schools and religious education programs.

5. To strengthen and support the Church: one's own parish community and parish priests; the worldwide Church and the Holy Father.

6. To do penance, including abstaining from meat and fasting from food on the appointed days.

7. To join in the missionary spirit and apostolate of the Church.

## The Theological Virtues

Faith          Hope          Charity (Love)

## The Cardinal Virtues

Prudence          Justice
Fortitude          Temperance

## Spiritual Works of Mercy

Admonish the sinner
Instruct the ignorant
Counsel the doubtful
Comfort the sorrowful
Bear wrongs patiently
Forgive all injuries
Pray for the living and the dead

## Corporal Works of Mercy

Feed the hungry
Give drink to the thirsty
Clothe the naked

Visit the imprisoned
Shelter the homeless
Visit the sick
Bury the dead

## The Gifts of the Holy Spirit

Wisdom
Understanding
Counsel
Fortitude

Knowledge
Piety
Fear of the Lord

## The Fruits of the Holy Spirit

Charity
Joy
Peace
Patience
Kindness
Goodness

Long-suffering
Humility
Fidelity
Modesty
Continence
Chastity

## The Seven Capital Sins

Pride
Covetousness
Lust
Anger

Gluttony
Envy
Sloth

## The Six Sins Against the Holy Spirit

1. Despair of one's salvation
2. Presumption of saving oneself without merit
3. Resisting the known truth
4. Envy of the graces received by others
5. Obstinacy in one's sins
6. Final impenitence

## The Four Sins that Cry to Heaven for Vengeance

1. Voluntary murder
2. The sin of impurity against nature
3. Taking advantage of the poor
4. Defrauding the workingman of his wages

## The Last Things

| | |
|---|---|
| Death | Heaven |
| Judgment | Hell |

## How To Baptize in Case of Emergency

Pour ordinary water on the forehead of the person to be baptized, and say while pouring it:

**"I baptize you in the name of the Father, and of the Son, and of the Holy Spirit."**

N.B. Any person of either sex, who has reached the use of reason, can and should baptize in case of necessity; the same person must say the words while pouring the water.

## How To Prepare for a Sick Call

Cover a small table with a white tablecloth. If possible, the table should be prepared near the bed so as to be within sight of the sick person. If customary, a vessel of holy water and a sprinkler or a small branch should be provided, as well as candles.

When the priest enters the house, he gives everyone a greeting of peace and then places the Blessed Eucharist on the table. All adore It. Then the priest sprinkles the sick person and the room with holy water, saying the prescribed prayer. The priest may then hear the sick person's confession. If sacramental confession is not part of the rite or if others are to receive Communion along with the sick person, the priest invites them to join in a penitential rite. A text from Scripture may then be read by one of those present or by the priest, who may explain the text. The Lord's Prayer follows. Then the priest distributes Holy Communion. A period of sacred silence may be observed. A concluding prayer and a blessing complete the Rite of Communion of the Sick.

## Sacrament of the Anointing of the Sick

We should call the priest in time when someone is in danger of death from sickness, accident or old age so that he may receive the grace and consolation from the Sacrament of Anointing of the Sick. In fact, Christ's minister should be called to visit the sick in any serious illness even when death does not seem near, because he will bring them the sacraments they need. Through His representative the divine Physician will come to the side of His suffering brother to be his strength and comfort.

Those who are in danger of death should be told of their condition so that they may prepare themselves to receive Christ in the sacraments worthily. It is false mercy to keep a very sick person ignorant of the fact that he may soon face God. Never wait until the person has lost consciousness or has gone into a coma before calling the priest.

In case of sudden or unexpected death, always call a priest, because absolution and the anointing can be given conditionally for some time after apparent death.

# BIBLIOGRAPHY

Alberione, James, S.S.P. *Blessed Are the Imitators of Mary Who Give Jesus to the World.* Boston: St. Paul Editions, 1982. Private publication.

_____.*Catechism for Adults.* Boston: St. Paul Editions, 1975.

Augustine, St. *The First Catechetical Instruction* in Ancient Christian Writers series. Translated by Joseph P. Christopher. Westminster, Md.: Newman Press, 1946.

Bonivento, Cesare, P.I.M.E., coordinator. *"Going Teach..."* Boston: St. Paul Editions, 1980.

Connell, Francis J., C.SS.R. *New Baltimore Catechism and Mass No. 3.* New York: Benziger Brothers, 1949.

Daughters of St. Paul. *Basic Catechism.* Boston: St. Paul Editions, 1980.

_____. *Religion for People of Today.* Boston: St. Paul Editions, 1971.

Documents of the Holy See. *Catechism of Modern Man.* Boston: St. Paul Editions, 1971.

_____. *Education.* Selected and arranged by the Benedictine Monks of Solesmes. Boston: St. Paul Editions, 1960.

_____. *Teaching the Catholic Faith Today* with Introduction by Eugene Kevane. Boston: St. Paul Editions, 1982.

Fox, Robert J. *Religious Education.* Boston: St. Paul Editions, 1972.

Gasparri, Peter Cardinal. *The Catholic Catechism.* New York: P. J. Kenedy and Sons, 1932.

Hardon, John A., S.J. *The Catholic Catechism.* Garden City, N.Y.: Doubleday and Co., 1975.

_____. *Modern Catholic Dictionary.* Garden City, N.Y.: Doubleday and Co., 1980.

_____. *The Question and Answer Catholic Catechism.* Garden City, N.Y.: Doubleday and Co., 1981.

Hofinger, Johannes, S.J. and Buckley, Francis J., S.J. *The Good News and Its Proclamation*. Notre Dame, Ind.: University of Notre Dame Press, 1968.

John Paul II, Pope. *Catechesi tradendae*. Boston: St. Paul Editions, 1979.

_____. *Familiaris consortio*. Boston: St. Paul Editions, 1981.

Jungmann, Joseph Andreas. *Handing on the Faith*. New York: Herder and Herder, 1959.

Kevane, Eugene. *Augustine the Educator*. Westminster, Md.: Newman Press, 1964.

_____. *Creed and Catechetics*. Boston: St. Paul Editions, 1983.

Lawler, Ronald, O.F.M. Cap., Wuerl, Donald W. and Lawler, Thomas C., editors. *The Teaching of Christ*. Huntington, Ind.: Our Sunday Visitor, 1976.

McHugh, John A., O.P. and Callan, Charles J., O.P. translators. *Catechism of the Council of Trent for Parish Priests*. Manila, Philippines: Sinag-tala Publishers, 1974.

McNicholas, John T., O.P. *This We Believe, By This We Live*. Patterson, N.J.: St. Anthony Guild Press, 1954.

Ott, Ludwig. *Fundamentals of Catholic Dogma*. St. Louis: B. Herder Book Co., 1954.

Paul VI, Pope. *Evangelii nuntiandi*. Boston: St. Paul Editions, 1976.

Pius X, Pope St. *Catechetical Documents of Pope Pius X*. Patterson, N.J.: St. Anthony Guild Press, 1946.

_____. *Catechism of Christian Doctrine*. Translated by Eugene Kevane. Middleburg, Va.: Notre Dame Institute Press, 1975.

Quasten, Johannes. *Patrology*. 3 volumes. Utrecht: Spectrum Publishers, 1966.

Sacred Congregation for the Clergy. *General Catechetical Directory*. Washington, D.C.: United States Catholic Conference, 1971.

Vatican Council II. *The Sixteen Documents of Vatican II*. Compiled by J. L. Gonzalez, S.S.P. and the Daughters of St. Paul. Boston: St. Paul Editions, 1967.

# Index

# For Your Family Library

The following books, magazines and pamphlets are available from any of the addresses at the back of this book.

# Adults

## Answers to Your Questions
Rev. Richard V. Lawlor, S.J.

There is no problem that faith cannot solve, no question that truth cannot answer. This timely volume contains inquiries sent in by readers of *The Family* magazine over a period of several years.

Covering topics such as prayer, morals, doctrine, marriage, ethics, and the Bible, a competent theologian provides in a concise but clear manner answers to *your* questions. This book is a helpful guide in confronting the prominent issues of our day—a book of answers in an age of questioning. 216 pages — RA0005

## Apostolic Exhortation on Catechesis in Our Time *(Catechesi tradendae)*
Pope John Paul II

The mission of handing on the Catholic Faith is presented clearly in this document of Pope John Paul II, emphasizing Jesus Christ, the heart of catechesis; the need of catechesis today; catechesis from the time of the Apostles; what is to be included in catechesis; the aim, ways and means of catechesis, and more. This is an excellent guide for every teacher of catechesis and every parent, as well as priests and bishops. 67 pages — EP0185

## The Bible for Everyone
Daughters of St. Paul

A complete Bible history, offering black and white art masters throughout. For individual or group study, for teens and adults, the entire Bible vividly unfolds—a marvelous introduction to the Scriptures. 352 pages — SC0020

## The Family—Center of Love and Life
Pope Paul VI, Pope John Paul I, Pope John Paul II
These messages regarding family life in the modern world reflect the particular role which the family is called to play in the entire plan of salvation. 361 pages — EP0484

## Fostering the Nobility of Marriage and the Family
This pamphlet is an excerpt from the Second Vatican Council's document, "Pastoral Constitution on the Church in the Modern World." 16 pages — PM0780

## Heaven
Daughters of St. Paul
As in a journey one keeps on thinking of the place he is headed for, so in this life's pilgrimage one must turn his mind toward the ultimate goal of his life—to his true country—heaven.

"Does heaven exist?"... "Has anyone ever come back from the dead to prove that there is a heaven?"... "How can we be sure that heaven exists?"

The present book answers these questions and also gives proofs to reassure those who might be wavering in their belief.

Heaven exists! All are called to that heavenly abode where unheard-of and eternal joys await us. 156 pages — SP0240

## In the Image of God
Sean O'Reilly, M.D.

Human sexuality is reflected upon within the context of its origin: the Triune God. The author's reverence, insight and knowledgeable conviction have produced a book that will lend itself to unlimited reflection by clergy, religious, parents and educators. And the book, acting as a spring-board, challenges the reader, according to his or her possibility, to spread far and wide a fundamental concept of Genesis: "God created man in his image..." (Gn. 1:27).

The author's vision extends beyond the con-fines of merely how to explain human sexuality to children. Inspired by a deep love for his Faith, and a desire to help reinforce two great papal docu-ments: *Of Human Life* by Pope Paul VI and *The Role of the Christian Family in the Modern World* by Pope John Paul II, Dr. Sean O'Reilly has written a work that will become for many a handbook they will go back to again and again. 92 pages — MS0308

## Lifetime of Love
S. L. Hart

The practical problems of everyday family liv-ing. Backed by the sound doctrine of Vatican II. Covers the whole span of married life—from the day of the wedding until "sunset." Newlyweds, in-laws, the budget, raising children, sex instruc-tion for little ones, divorce, birth control, family cooperation, the role of mother and father, teen-agers, growing old together—these and countless more topics are in this complete, up-to-date mar-riage manual. 534 pages — MS0350

**Morality Today**—The Bible in My Life
Daughters of St. Paul

A unique way to study the ten commandments!

In simple and clear language, but with a very personal approach, each commandment is explained in all its aspects, negative and positive. We are invited to ponder...adore...and speak to God so that through instruction, reflection and prayer we may understand and love His holy law.

All will find this book both informative and inspirational. 167 pages — SC0088

**Natural Family Planning**—the 100% Solution
Fr. Herbert F. Smith, S.G.; Dr. Joseph M. Gambescia, M.D. and Albert Vera

This relevant pamphlet by experts delineates the advantages of using the God-given ways of family planning. 30 pages — PM1315

**The Role of the Christian Family in the Modern World** (*Familiaris consortio*)
Pope John Paul II

Showing his characteristic love and solicitude for the "domestic Church"—the family—Pope John Paul II speaks on timely issues such as: the situation of the family today, God's plan for marriage and the family, the transmission of life, the education of children, the family as the cell of society, the role of each member of the family, evangelization in the family, the family and the sacraments, and pastoral care of the family. 139 pages — EP0973

**Secrets for Finding Happiness in Marriage**
Valentino Del Mazza

"Getting married is easy, but living together happily with a love which endures the trials of time is a lifelong art." In this handy volume are found practical and encouraging suggestions for developing, deepening and even regaining true happiness in marriage. The author covers not only the relationship between husband and wife, but between parents and children, between the family and society.

Developing his points with concrete examples from the lives of other married couples, Del Mazza explains clearly how to attain harmony in marriage. Invaluable, too, are excerpts taken from inspiring messages given by Pope John Paul II to married and engaged couples.

Applicable for every stage of married life, this is a book that will be used again and again. 90 pages — MS0632

## Spiritual Life in the Bible
Daughters of St. Paul

A volume which pursues the truth about a wealth of timely and fundamental subjects.

Written in a form of dialogue, the author continually draws from the Book of books—the Bible—whose Author is God, the Author of Truth and the true Light of the world.

A book which will be of interest to both those who believe in objective truth, and those who honestly seek to pursue the truth. 456 pages — SC0445

## Successful Parenting
Ann M. and John F. Murphy

Raising children can be exciting and rewarding; however, sometimes it becomes frightening and frustrating. When parents become positive in their outlook, loving in their attitude, and kind in their actions, then raising boys and girls can become a most rewarding, worthwhile, lifetime accomplishment. In this book the authors share their parenting research, methods, and philosophy with the reader. 264 pages — MS0657

## Vatican II Sunday Missal

Prepared by the Daughters of St. Paul

This is a complete, up-to-date, perpetual missal, including explanations of the Scriptural readings; all the Sunday Masses, as well as holy days of obligation and other feasts; the Order of Mass; prayers; a liturgical calendar and a concise but clear instruction on the Catholic way of life. 1,120 pages — MS0740P, paperback; MS0740C, cloth; MS0750, leatherette; MS0760, leather

## Vatican II Weekday Missal

Prepared by the Daughters of St. Paul

All the weekday readings, the proper and common of saints, ritual Masses, votive Masses, and Masses for the dead are found in this one volume missal, as well as brief profiles of each saint, daily meditations and biblical introductions. 2,400 pages — MS0770, cloth; MS0780, leatherette; MS0790, leather

## Woman: Her Influence and Zeal

Rev. James Alberione, SSP, STD

The challenging role of the Christian woman is forcefully described by the Servant of God, Fr. James Alberione. Various apostolates of the woman are shown, with a special emphasis on how woman's mission assists the priesthood. "The book is dominated by one fundamental idea and it is this: Woman was destined to be man's helpmate, not just materially but spiritually as well.

This latter function she can only accomplish if she is truly religious, both in outlook and action."
—from the Prologue 316 pages — MS0820

## Yes to Life
Edited by the Daughters of St. Paul

An invaluable source-book bringing together the consistent teaching of the Church through the centuries on the sacredness of human life.

Here in one volume is proclaimed the fundamental truth of the value of all human life in the words of the Fathers of the Church, the Popes, Vatican II and the bishops of our day. 330 pages — EP1110

# *Teenagers*

## Give Your Life with Joy
Pope Paul VI and Pope John Paul II

In an age of comfort and self-satisfaction, of pleasure and independence, the poor, chaste and obedient Jesus has lost none of His appeal for generous youth. They are capable of *giving* to God and the Church not only minutes or hours but a *lifetime* in the priestly or religious vocation.

Whether one is considering the call, guiding young people, or already in the Lord's service, this book offers rich insights and warm encouragement. Its message, expressed today by Christ's Vicars— Pope Paul VI and Pope John Paul II—was once voiced by the Divine Master Himself: "Come, follow me." Blessed are those privileged to answer, and to give their lives with joy. 92 pages — EP0515

## I Believe in Youth, Christ Believes in Youth
Pope John Paul II

Sequel to *You Are the Future, You Are My Hope*. *I Believe in Youth, Christ Believes in Youth* is a

volume that breathes hope, confidence, joy and challenge. The young and all who deal with them in any way will find in these pages reassuring direction and secure strength for life.

Jesus and His Gospel are presented as the source and goal of all desires and activities. Personality, careers, states in life, pains and sorrows, joys and successes—all converge in the attractive Person of Jesus Christ.

The young will feel that they are indeed loved and trusted, and that they are capable of valiant responses to this love and trust.

*I Believe in Youth, Christ Believes in Youth* is this "electrical charge" of confidence needed by our young people, and, indeed, by all persons today. 297 pages — EP0586

## Looking Ahead to Marriage

Daughters of St. Paul

From the most sublime to the most practical, *Looking Ahead to Marriage* delves into the meaning of the marriage commitment. Comprehensive material on every aspect of engagement and married life itself. Partial contents: Love, what is it?; premarital chastity; parental advice or opposition; emotions; sacramental grace; the Church's teaching on birth control; working mothers; communicating; sharing. 336 pages — CA0120

## Teenagers and Purity—
## Teenagers and Going Steady—
## Teenagers Looking Toward Marriage

Rev. Robert J. Fox

Based on the Vatican's "Declaration on Sexual Ethics," this booklet is a simple but valuable presentation of the Catholic outlook on sexuality.

It is directed to teenagers in a style that is at once clear and encouraging, informative and uplifting. 62 pages — MS0660

## Teenagers Today
A Friend of Youth

What makes for happiness? What is the truth about drugs, popularity, sex? How does one go about forming a balanced character, acquiring virtue, and choosing a state in life? All this and much more are covered in this practical and realistic volume.

*Teenagers Today* is written by a friend of youth, who has spent years sharing experiences and growing in genuine love for the "hope of tomorrow."

This book will be read and reread by teenagers as well as parents, teachers, counselors, and all those who are concerned with today's youth, molding tomorrow's adults. 168 pages — MS0665

## "You Are the Future, You Are My Hope"
Pope John Paul II
Compiled and indexed by the Daughters of St. Paul

Volume one of the talks of His Holiness *to young people*. Reveals the stirring personal appeal of the Pope to the new generation. Excellent for youth and those involved in guidance. 326 pages; 16 pages of full-color photos — EP1120

## Your Right To Be Informed
Daughters of St. Paul

Directed to the teenager, this book also finds many parents and other adults among its readers! Relevant, complete development of topics such as

God, man, life of Christ, temperaments, conscience, morals—in simple, clear language. Its positive and optimistic approach to life is irresistible. 432 pages — CA0090

## *Children*
### Encounter Books

"African Triumph" — St. Charles Lwanga EN0010

"Ahead of the Crowd" — St. Dominic Savio EN0020

"Bells of Conquest" — St. Bernard of Clairvaux EN0030

"Boy with a Mission" — Francis Marto EN0040

"Came the Dawn" — Blessed Mother EN0045

"Catherine of Siena" — St. Catherine of Siena EN0050

"The Cheerful Warrior" — St. Charles Garnier EN0060

"The Conscience Game" — St. Thomas More EN0070

"The Country Road Home" — St. John Vianney EN0080

"The Fisher Prince" — St. Peter EN0090

"Flame in the Night" — St. Francis Xavier EN0100

"Footsteps of a Giant" — St. Charles Borromeo EN0110

"A Gamble for God" — St. Camillus de Lellis EN0118

"Gentle Revolutionary" — St. Francis of Assisi EN0120

"Girl in the Stable" — St. Germaine EN0130

"God's Secret Agent" — Father Michael Pro, S.J. EN0140

"The Great Hero" — St. Paul EN0150

## Fifty-Seven Saints for Boys and Girls
Daughters of St. Paul

Some of the saints in these stories did great things; others did only ordinary things. Yet they all bear a "family resemblance" because the likeness of Christ was produced in each one of them. They all spoke with God often in prayer, tried to keep the ten commandments perfectly, and were kind and helpful to their fellowmen. Every child or young teenager who reads these personal, simple stories will be drawn to imitate these heroes of God and take them as their heavenly protectors. 581 pages — CH0210

## Growing Up
M. Josephine Colville

Rhymes to help in the guidance of young children, all based on practical Christian psychology and experience.

"Having a heart for others
Means that yours must be a prize
No matter how you're little
There's no telling of its size."

168 pages — MS0264

## I Learn About Jesus
Daughters of St. Paul

A pre-schooler's very own book about Jesus! Beginning with the joyous invitation to see the action of God in the wonders of our world, these colorful pages help youngsters learn about their loving Savior and ever-present Friend. Richly illustrated with full-color drawings and appealing children's photos. 144 pages — CA0240T

## Jesus in the Gospel
Compiled by the Daughters of St. Paul

This beautifully bound volume will help children learn more about Jesus and about how He proved His love for each of us. The life, teaching, death and resurrection of Jesus come alive throughout the pages of *Jesus in the Gospel*, all in the words of the Gospel. This special book has over 135 full-color pictures. 304 pages — CH0288

## Little Stories About God
Mary Reynolds McDonald

The whole biblical story delightfully retold in a child's language by a mother of five children. "Where does God live?" "What does He do all day?" and countless other questions which children ask can be answered so simply with this book. This Bible for little ones (ages 3-6) is marvelously illustrated with full-color pictures on almost every page. 134 pages — CH0330

## The Teachings and Miracles of Jesus
Daughters of St. Paul

Some of the best-known teachings and miracles of our Lord are retold in this volume for young people. Jesus has an answer to every question; He has words of everlasting life. His tender love for people and His divine power will strike unforgettable images on the minds and hearts of youth to aid them to work for His kingdom. Illustrated with beautiful full-color pictures. 136 pages — CH0690

# For the Whole Family
## Basic Catechism
Daughters of St. Paul

This concise, direct book presents the fundamentals of the Catholic Faith in a question-and-answer format with related scriptural quotations.

Thoroughly indexed for ready reference, it is a vital handbook for anyone desiring to deepen or clarify his belief. 208 pages — RA0007

## The Eternal Wisdom
Rev. James Alberione, SSP, STD

Often called a one-book encyclopedia of the Catholic Faith—a brilliant four-color art master accompanies each page of explanation with Scripture references throughout. An ideal family book and convert manual. 180 pages — RA0090

## Periodicals
### The Family

Published monthly (except bi-monthly July-August). It contains:

—Spiritually enriching features for every member of the family

—Intriguing lives of saints

—Optimistic spotlights on the world

—Articles on Scripture

—Response to readers' religious or moral questions

—Thoughts of the Pope

—Psychology from a practical Christian viewpoint

—Religious education for children and the family

—Contemporary prayers, inspirational verses, page for young people, movie reviews, photo album, and much, much more!

### My Friend

The ideal magazine for children!

For ages 6-12; 32 pages of fun and learning, including:

—Bible stories

—Beautiful lives of the saints

—Contests

—Projects

—Science articles

—And many other features which will keep children involved.

Comes out every month (except July and August).

## Strain Forward

The magazine with depth! An excellent help for deepening the spiritual life. Published monthly, (except bi-monthly July-August), *Strain Forward* contains:

—Sunday Liturgy Themes

—Talks of the Pope to bishops, priests, religious, seminarians and all the People of God

—Thoughts and reflections for spiritual growth.

### The Daughters of St. Paul

It has been said that if St. Paul were to return to the earth, he would use the modern and efficacious means of communication to preach the Word of God.

In 1953, His Holiness, Pope Pius XII, blessed, praised and approved the modern congregation, the Pious Society of the *Daughters of St. Paul,* which is dedicated to the spreading of the Faith by using the apostolate of the press, radio, television and motion pictures, as St. Paul, their father, would have done.

These modern media are a most effective means of reaching souls. They have become a terrible weapon in the hands of Satan; they must be a powerful sword and shield for the Church to promote the kingdom of Jesus Christ.

The Daughters of St. Paul offer their daily prayers, sacrifices and labor in reparation for the sins committed through bad literature, films and programs, and they endeavor to replace these with *good,* wholesome literature, films, TV and radio programs. These Sisters write, print, bind, broadcast and film the Word of God.

The literature from their presses as well as their films are distributed by the Sisters themselves through their *St. Paul Catholic Book and Film Centers* and also by "house-to-house" distribution—a technique they know has never failed, the very technique their patron, St. Paul, employed.

The Daughters of St. Paul carry out their important apostolate in 32 nations. Their congregation is young—founded in 1915 by Very Reverend James Alberione, S.S.P., S.T.D., and their Co-Foundress, the Servant of God, Mother Thecla Merlo. St. Paul, the Apostle, is their Protector. In imitation of him, therefore, the Daughters of St. Paul strive to zealously and generously dedicate all their energies to the work of sanctifying themselves and winning many souls to God.

...it has been said that it was work...
...returning the verb, it would use the...
...the text and all because of the...
communication to preach the Word of God...
in 1955. His Holiness Pope Pius XII...
"blessed, praised and approved the most...
...congregation, that this Society of the...
Daughters of St. Paul will be dedicated...
...to the spreading of the Faith by making...
available of the press, radio, television,
...motion pictures, etc.'... Such men...
rather would have done...

These modern media were most effective
instruments of reaching souls. They have
the same standards both in the frame of
Salamanca and as a powerful sword that
"stand for the Church's battle on the King's
Son of David in Christ...

The Daughters of St. Paul offer their daily prayers, sacrifices and
their open-air exhortations also through the through out the United States and
..in progress... They endeavour to reach those who do not...
welcome some frequent... through TV and radio programs... those online...
..used with time, the book centre and the Word of God...

The first are, from these presses as well as through the home
..have directly the Sisters themselves, throughout... St. Paul Catholic
Book and Film Centres and also by house-to-house distribution...
techniques they know has never failed the very message we're carrying...
to every household...

The Daughters of St. Paul carry out their apostolate related to the
...nations. Their congregation in peace... founded in 1915 by Very
Reverend James Alberione S.S.P. S.T.D. and their Co-Foundress...
the heroism of Our Mother Thecla Merlo of Paul the Apostle is now...
Therefore, in imitation of their ancestor, our ancestors of St. Paul
strive to zealously and passionately to teach all their people, to the
work of sanctifying themselves, and winning many souls to God...

# Daughters of St. Paul

**IN MASSACHUSETTS**
50 St. Paul's Ave., Jamaica Plain, Boston, MA 02130; **617-522-8911.**
172 Tremont Street, Boston, MA 02111; **617-426-5464; 617-426-4230.**

**IN NEW YORK**
78 Fort Place, Staten Island, NY 10301; **212-447-5071; 212-447-5086.**
59 East 43rd Street, New York, NY 10017; **212-986-7580.**
625 East 187th Street, Bronx, NY 10458; **212-584-0440.**
525 Main Street, Buffalo, NY 14203; **716-847-6044.**

**IN NEW JERSEY**
Hudson Mall—Route 440 and Communipaw Ave.,
Jersey City, NJ 07304; **201-433-7740.**

**IN CONNECTICUT**
202 Fairfield Ave., Bridgeport, CT 06604; **203-335-9913.**

**IN OHIO**
2105 Ontario Street (at Prospect Ave.), Cleveland, OH 44115;
**216-621-9427.**
25 E. Eighth Street, Cincinnati, OH 45202; **513-721-4838;
513-421-5733.**

**IN PENNSYLVANIA**
1719 Chestnut Street, Philadelphia, PA 19103; **215-568-2638.**

**IN VIRGINIA**
1025 King Street, Alexandria, VA 22314; **703-683-1741; 703-549-3806.**

**IN FLORIDA**
2700 Biscayne Blvd., Miami, FL 33137; **305-573-1618.**

**IN LOUISIANA**
4403 Veterans Memorial Blvd., Metairie, LA 70002; **504-887-7631;
504-887-0113.**
1800 South Acadian Thruway, P.O. Box 2028, Baton Rouge, LA 70821;
**504-343-4057; 504-381-9485.**

**IN MISSOURI**
1001 Pine Street (at North 10th), St. Louis, MO 63101; **314-621-0346;
314-231-1034.**

**IN ILLINOIS**
172 North Michigan Ave., Chicago, IL 60601; **312-346-4228;
312-346-3240.**

**IN TEXAS**
114 Main Plaza, San Antonio, TX 78205; **512-224-8101; 512-224-0938.**

**IN CALIFORNIA**
1570 Fifth Ave., San Diego, CA 92101; **619-232-1442.**
46 Geary Street, San Francisco, CA 94108; **415-781-5180.**

**IN WASHINGTON**
2301 Second Ave., Seattle, WA 98121.

**IN HAWAII**
1143 Bishop Street, Honolulu, HI 96813; **808-521-2731.**

**IN ALASKA**
750 West 5th Ave., Anchorage, AK 99501; **907-272-8183.**

**IN CANADA**
3022 Dufferin Street, Toronto 395, Ontario, Canada.

**IN ENGLAND**
199 Kensington High Street, London W8 63A, England.
133 Corporation Street, Birmingham B4 6PH, England.
5A-7 Royal Exchange Square, Glasgow G1 3AH, England.
82 Bold Street, Liverpool L1 4HR, England.

**IN AUSTRALIA**
58 Abbotsford Rd., Homebush, N.S.W. 2140, Australia.